WALK OF THE CENTIPEDE

A STORY OF ONE MAN'S JOURNEY THROUGH CATASTROPHIC INJURY

JAY CLARK AND AURA SANCHEZ GARFUNKEL

iUNIVERSE, INC.
NEW YORK BLOOMINGTON

Walk of the Centipede
A Story of One Man's Journey through Catastrophic Injury

iUniverse books may be ordered through booksellers or by contacting:

iUniverse
1663 Liberty Drive
Bloomington, IN 47403
www.iuniverse.com
1-800-Authors (1-800-288-4677)

Because of the dynamic nature of the Internet, any Web addresses or links contained in this book may have changed since publication and may no longer be valid.

ISBN: 978-1-4502-2215-0 (sc)
ISBN: 978-1-4502-2217-4 (dj)
ISBN: 978-1-4502-2216-7 (ebk)

Printed in the United States of America

iUniverse rev. date: 6/25/2010

To Frank,

whose desire to discover the truth
of the matter marked his life.

CONTENTS

PREFACE

This story is about Frank Garfunkel's struggle to regain a measure of control over his life after a paralyzing accident. At age sixty-four Frank damaged his spinal cord, resulting in quadriplegia, a condition he interpreted and articulated for others until his death six years later. It is also our story, Aura's as his wife, advocate and primary caretaker; and Jay's as a friend who joined with Frank in a series of tape-recorded conversations about his daily encounters with failure and triumph in the hospital.

We met frequently over a period of six years to produce this volume. As we edited the transcripts and discussed the context in which to present them, we risked becoming lost in the immensity of the material—not only the great number of written and transcribed pieces but also the feelings and memories they evoked. We wondered whether to include our own experiences, and finally decided that our written accounts – both prose pieces and poems – would provide the context we sought for Frank's spoken words. Frequently we wondered who our audience would be. At the beginning we thought it might be students training to work in the health professions; at another point, family members of patients undergoing long hospital stays. Ultimately, the story that emerged was about a person engaged in regaining mastery over his environment, both the one in which he was living as well as the internal world of body and mind.

Jay Clark and Aura Sanchez Garfunkel

A note on transcripts:

In his opening comment to Jay, Frank cites the power of pain and illness to isolate. So powerful is it that he must choose: yield to torment's enclosure or ignore it in order to go on living. Thus Frank describes the gulf he experiences between himself and the healthy, recorded in these conversations. Though supported by family and friends, the extremity of his challenge often causes him to feel alone in an alien world, fighting to conquer his chaotic nervous system and the rigidity of institutional expectations.

It is grimly ironic that at the moment when we stand in the greatest need of support from others, serious illness or injury often limits our access to those who respect and love us. So arresting can be the experience of pain that one is thrust into a chasm of existential uncertainty that is rarely articulated. As he struggled to fathom his condition, Frank not only deemed it important not only to speak of his travail with a friend, but also to record these struggles. Regular opportunities to talk with Jay allowed Frank to recreate himself, not as patient or victim, but rather as narrator of his odyssey and partner in the give and take of wide ranging dialogue.

Frank and Jay recorded their conversations in Frank's room at the rehabilitation hospital during the evening hours, usually after visitors had left and before final preparations were made by the nursing staff for Frank to go to sleep. After Frank returned to his home in Winthrop, he, Jay, and occasionally, Aura conversed in Frank's bedroom on the first floor, the site of the family's former dining room. Except where noted, these conversations also occurred in the late evening before Frank went to sleep.

Jay Clark and Aura Sanchez Garfunkel
Winthrop, Massachusetts, 2010

ACKNOWLEDGEMENTS

We are grateful to Elena Harap who edited the manuscript and helped us distinguish between the occasional ramblings of conversation and passages that illuminated fundamental struggles. Her eye for the essential disclosed to us the power of the reflections with which we were working and renewed our desire to see our project through to completion.

We also wish to express our gratitude to Marie Pappas for encouraging us to include our stories. Her suggestion that we view our own narratives and poems, together with the transcripts themselves, as pieces that could be arranged as a collage to tell the story freed us at a point when we were groping for an organizational frame of reference.

We are indebted to Dr. Victor Kestenbaum of the Boston University Department of Philosophy who read our completed manuscript and affirmed our belief that Frank's account of his ordeal provided a unique and valuable narrative, capturing the profound sense of isolation brought about by pain in cases of extreme trauma.

We are also grateful to Anelisa Garfunkel, Frank and Aura's daughter, for helping to select and digitize the photos for this book, working on the cover, and giving us invaluable feedback at various stages of manuscript development. Anelisa, a filmmaker, used some of Frank's conversations in a short documentary entitled

One Hundred Steps. This film is available through her web site: Ropeswingfilms.com.

We wish to express our appreciation to Frank's sister, Charlotte Snyder, and to a number of his close friends, including Alex Rodriguez, Ed Boyd, Bob and Nan Archer, and Alex Alexanian, who supplied vital information for Aura's biographical piece on Frank's years before his injury.

On numerous occasions Thornton Shepherd was extremely helpful to us as we struggled to prepare the manuscript for printing. We are deeply grateful for his kind assistance.

We thank Micha Archer for her understanding of Frank, expressed through the artistry and power of our cover.

Finally we wish to thank the members of our families: Kitty, David, Judean, Chloe, Sadie and Peter Clark; and Dylan Monahan, and Seth and Anelisa Garfunkel whose support sustained us while we worked on the manuscript.

INTRODUCTION

Reading maketh a full man, conference a ready man, and writing an exact man.

Francis Bacon, from the essay,
"Of Studies", 1625

In these pages we allow Frank, the main character, to speak with his own voice. After his accident Frank had proposed that he and Jay talk regularly, that their conversations be tape recorded and eventually transcribed. In doing so, he created an unusual and compelling legacy; a *first-person* account of day-to-day experience of the physical pain and helplessness associated with a severe spinal cord injury. Frank also explored the feelings of powerlessness he and Aura encountered in dealing with physicians and staff at the rehabilitation hospital. He spoke of his growing sense that the progress of recovery was slowly eroding. While others experiencing hospitalization have encountered similar trauma, we are not aware of first-person accounts that probe so deeply the journey into catastrophic injury, extended hospitalization and return home.

Most of Frank's hospital time was spent with doctors and staff or alone in his room rather than with colleagues, family and friends. Deprived of the interactive flow that most of us in the outside world enjoy, Frank regarded talks with visitors as a respite from his hospitalization. He explained to Jay that he didn't want to weigh friends and colleagues down with the depth of his trials, lest they be driven away. Accordingly he reserved for Aura and for Jay the most painful, frightening and discouraging aspects of his experience.

The limits of conversation are usually spontaneous. In Frank's case they were established by the hospital's visiting hours or the fatigue arising from medication, pain, or physical or occupational therapy sessions. Thus the transcribed conversations often end with Frank's saying he is ready to go to sleep, in some cases, his drifting off to sleep, or in others, of the tape running out.

As Bacon's statement implies, spoken words tend to be less polished than writing. In addition, at least two people control the conversation resulting in unpredictability. These characteristics lend spontaneity to the transcripts but also an element of randomness; here, we have edited tangents, redundancies and awkward phrasings in order to maintain a coherent narrative. Our own experiences are interspersed with the transcripts of twenty conversations to form a collage, telling the story of Frank's trauma and his spiritual recovery. We have also included, in several installments, a biography of Frank.

Walk of the Centipede is arranged into four parts that cover Frank's injury, his nearly three months of hospitalization, and his return home. Part V reflects on events following the four-month period of transcriptions and ends with Frank's death nearly six years later. Each of the first four parts is introduced with a brief synopsis of highlights from the conversations. In Part V Aura and Jay look back on Frank's life following his hospitalization.

Frank's story is not a Hollywood, larger-than-life fable of a hero overcoming disability against all odds. It is not an air-brushed photograph that hides the wrinkles of fear or the warts of deep depression. It is the story of vulnerability, trauma, suffering, depression, existential absurdity and bewilderment – side by side with laughter, euphoria, gratitude, amazement and love. His primary doctor once said to him, "I don't know how you do it. You're such a strong person. I don't think I could." Frank responded, "It's not like you'd have a choice."

PART I: THE UNEXPECTED

During his first conversation on September 29, Frank speaks with Jay about how disorienting his experience has been, from losing sensation, mobility and independence, to requiring medication—in short, entering the world of the hospital. A professor and former department head, he now finds himself excluded from the decision-making process. At the same time Frank begins to weave the two disparate parts of his life together: one as a hospitalized patient and the other as an advocate for the rights of the handicapped.

FRANK AND JAY, TUESDAY, SEPTEMBER 29, 1992: "I WAS A MESS"

Jay: Well, we're finally doing it after all this time.

Frank: All the words that I have been spewing out the last four weeks and two days, what's happened to me, what's happened to the people around me—and yet I was unable to write about it because I don't have the hands to write, unable to dictate because I just didn't have the will. One way is to talk with you, Jay, about certain questions or issues that seemed to be quite important.

Jay: It really feels that part of the healing is talking about it, not only for you but for everybody else, for people who may listen to this or read it in the future. Just talking with Aura tonight, I realized that the staff in the institution here don't know what this experience is like.

Frank: And people who go through the experience forget it. So that they can live with themselves. They forget what the nights were like, what the waiting and waiting and waiting was about. They forget about the pain, the, at times, hopelessness of it. Even my first week at the [medical hospital] is a total blur now. I remember bits and pieces: nurses; and the bed; and trying to get another bed because the first bed was so uncomfortable. And coming to the realization that it was not the bed at all, it was that my muscles had taken a trip, an acid trip, and were confused. Some weren't working, some were partially working. It was like having cement blocks, steel bands around my stomach, and pieces of wood along my spine, none of which had anything to do with reality.

Jay: Sounds like when you first came to the hospital, you expected the changes could be made because they were external to you, and that part of the settling in was realizing that some of those conditions were internal. There was confusion about where changes could or couldn't be made.

Frank: I remember the first reaction I had when I was still on the squash court, recalling times when somehow my arm would pop out and suddenly feel again. I was waiting for this pop or this feeling to come back, or the temporary shock to disappear, and I would be whole again. Then it became clear that I wasn't whole, I was a mess. Then I didn't know whether anything was broken. Somehow I have a memory of a broken neck figuring into it. It was scary, painful, and mysterious all bound up into one fused blob.

Jay: (noticing Frank trying to reach the pad that had slipped off his elbow) Do you want your elbow covered?

Frank: This one? Yes. Some of the overriding feelings I had throughout this had to do with the strangeness of different culture, different country. When I watched television, I would always be surprised when I saw Boston weather or a Boston traffic report or Boston sports. It was like I would be in some foreign country, in Yugoslavia, and suddenly I would see a Boston traffic report. It didn't make any sense to me.

Jay: Even now?

Frank: Yeah and when I'm just gaining consciousness or dozing I see the Bunker Hill monument and wonder what the hell it's doing here. I get the idea that I'm in some big building in some strange city in some strange country, that I don't belong here. The people are different. I guess this is the same thing as when people talk about the culture of disability, that it separates, it confines, it isolates and works against rejoining or becoming again part of whatever you were a part of before it happened.

Jay: It's really striking to hear that that is your personal experience, over and above whatever the institution does either to include or not include you as a person. The institution can help to make you part of the world or exclude you from it.

Frank: But I guess that's the question: what are the things that go towards isolation and separation, temporary or permanent, to people in here, and what are the things that really encourage one to be part of whatever one was doing in the community in the life outside. I can think of the fact that it is easy to come and park for free here as being an integrating factor. I can think of the fact that when you get here, even though they have visiting hours, I have never seen anyone be asked to leave at any time. On the other hand, the fact they have a telephone service where you really can't call out is an isolating factor. Furthermore, if someone calls you and the phone rings and you don't or can't answer it, no one does, and that's the end of it. So they have a mixed system. Some parts contribute to making it easy for visitors to come and stay, and others make it very difficult to maintain contacts.

Jay: There is a sort of schizophrenic quality to that: on one hand inviting you to be part of the community of friends you have, but on the other hand, this business with the phone.

Frank: One of the biggest things that happened to me, since I have practically no use of my hands, is that I became totally dependent on people for everything: eating, dressing, moving my body around my bed and brushing my teeth. There are a lot of things that my hands are good enough to do if the right equipment were here, the right switches, the right paraphernalia. But they weren't here. None of it started to appear until either I had it brought in from the outside, like my telephone, or I made the point to the occupational therapist. "Look, I can't turn the television on and I can't adjust it." Then she worked on it and eventually put the switches in such a way that I could work them. I couldn't raise myself in the bed or turn my light on or off. Unless I got someone into this room or someone was with me, I had to live with whatever it was. That was strange; it meant I couldn't control anything. I couldn't control my life as it was.

Jay: You were a stranger to yourself in some ways, just from both the physical and the emotional nature of the experience. But you also arrived here as a stranger to them. With negotiation, fighting, teaching and dialogue that estrangement has reduced itself to some extent, but it's in itself remarkable that you arrive here a stranger to the organization. You could say that you are not like most of the people here in terms of the nature of your problems but still —

Frank: —but neither is anyone else. Everyone is so different here, people who are amputees, each one of them has totally different issues from the next. All of the spinal cord cases, maybe eight, ten, twelve people—to take all of them and lump them together is maybe medically or anatomically valid, but it certainly is not psychologically valid. People who have had strokes, again each one is different. But they use medical designations and lump them together on floors; the stroke victims on one, spinal cord on another, a pain floor, a pediatric floor, and these distinctions are really very artificial.

Jay: They're just like any other label.

Frank: Yes, they serve a medical purpose; they don't serve a psychological or cultural purpose.

Jay: Well, they serve a psychological and cultural purpose for the organization, which has a need to maintain its stability in the face of the idiosyncrasies of the patients who come in.

Frank: Yeah, they have what they call social groups on this floor and I never have gone to any of them, they don't seem particularly appropriate. I walk [sic] into the social group and there are people who have different needs and different interests. But there are people in this building who I would find very interesting to talk to. I accidentally met a lawyer on the fourth floor, and a professor on another floor; there are people in this building who it would be natural to get together and talk with. It would be natural for them to be treated in a similar way, as people who are continuing their careers, who have certain needs, like reading; but they are all separated because one has had a stroke and one has a spinal condition, and nothing is done to compensate for that.

Jay: In other words, the medical distinctions prevail rather than those that could make a real difference in terms of the social, emotional, cognitive or other aspects of people's recovery.

Frank: Well, say for medical reasons there is a specialist in spinal cord injuries on this floor. That means you're going to see that person every day and have access to that person anytime. I found it to be a great advantage that such a physician is on this floor; she gives me her time whenever I need it and she's always available and I don't have to go all over the building to find her. If the other physicians are doing what she is doing, they could really survey their patients and find out a lot about them, what their interests are: whether they play chess, are readers or have an interest in computers or have common intellectual, professional or business interests. They could give people an opportunity to know who else is here, who you might be able to talk to. But nothing like that is done.

Jay: As you describe your experience it has physical overtones, yes, but the predominant ones are existential. They're ones of where you belong in the world—

Frank: Yeah.

Jay: —and they are crucial to survival to survival mentally and emotionally. They are also crucial to recovery. Key parts of your survival are idiosyncratic but the staff are not reaching out to listen to that. Yet that seems to make a powerful difference in terms of what does one do when one is disoriented. You probably have more people visiting you than ninety-nine percent of the other patients here. They have been a vital source of life flow for you. But what does someone do who has one or two visitors and whose life or death almost, is going to depend on that.

Frank: What comes to mind, going back to your statement about the schizophrenia of the place, is that most of the staff here are focused on the physiological, the anatomical, and the neurological ingredients of cure or not cure. You will get better if your body works right, if you get the right physical therapy, the right medicines and maybe the right surgery. They talk about motivated patients who really want to get better, who work hard to get better and are looking for more therapy, but I think there is strong aspect of the belief system here which says, 'yeah, that's good to have motivated patients, but what's really at issue is neurological, anatomic, physiological things'. This psychiatrist who I've met seems to represent a minority view that part of the treatment is going to be motivation. It's going to be a belief in being able to get better. As you look closely at the place, there's all kinds of evidence of both things going on at the same time.

Jay: It seems to me that the medical model, which is what you are describing, is the linear model; it's the traditional, western, find the quickest route from-A-to-B, logically based, data based to some extent. But it's different from a systemic approach which says that there are many factors that influence an outcome. This latter approach has a more speculative, exploratory quality. Do you want something?

Frank: I just want to turn around a little bit.

Jay: I think that linear and systemic mentalities represent radically different ways of looking at the world. The way the hospital looks at it seems to be that other factors may influence a patient's recovery, but that attention to them must not undermine the central concern, the physiological care of a patient.

Frank: Yeah, that's illustrated by the fact that you don't participate in decisions, you aren't presented with options. As a matter of fact, I asked one of the occupational therapists what were some of the controversies in her field. She didn't know what I meant by that. Now I don't know, but I could guess that there are some very different philosophies in occupational and physical therapy, as well as in all kinds of treatment aspects for disease, for spinal injuries. And yet they're not living with that controversy; they've simply been taught in the university, in some hospitals, and in some clinic someplace what good procedure is. To think that they don't know what the controversies are is to suggest that they would not know how to present options to you. Therefore those meetings with you are unnecessary. (chuckles)

Jay: If they sat down and talked with you, they would find out how vital controversy is to your way of testing a cognitive or a social system. If you don't find controversy, you immediately smell a rat. So here they are, presenting you with simplistic, non-controversial models. You can trust the staff, but there's a certain level at which they can't communicate with you.

Frank: Right, that's a big difference. That's what separates us. And when we introduce controversy into it, it turns into confrontation and a rejection of them. Not of their ideas but of them as people, as professionals.

Jay: While that may be so, it sounds as if some of the confrontation has led to real dialogue, some discussion of how to handle you.

Frank: Yeah, most recently I had a computer I was using and it turned out I couldn't use the computer unless the therapist was there. And yet I knew more about how to use the computer than anyone I met here. They told me it was a rule; therefore, I couldn't use the computer late afternoons, evenings, weekends or during the day when I had down time. So I raised it as an issue and immediately they turned around on it, and said, "Well, there's another computer you can use and we'll give you permission to use that anytime when it's not being used by anyone else". It's on the eighth floor in a really nice space. So, they quickly gave in on that.

Jay: They gave in, but they did it by finding another computer. So they didn't have to break the rule.

Frank: Right, right. Of course, when I get to the computer, it's not at all equipped. It's a computer for able-bodied people. In fact, someone has remarked to me that this is a hospital for able-bodied people. (laughter) There's no way I can press the elevator buttons to go to any other floor. And I've tried every which way to press those buttons. All their bed switches— can't use any of them because they don't lend themselves to someone who has the kind of hands I have.

Well maybe, going back to my earlier point, everyone is so different in so many ways that if they tried to provide for individual differences it would be astronomically expensive. As you walk through the halls and find out about who is here, it's very striking that they will take almost anyone who has had a serious injury or a serious disease, anything that doesn't require an acute care hospital. The person can be six, sixty or ninety; there is a ninety-one year old man who is being rehabilitated. And there are many patients who, much of the time, refuse to talk to the therapist or have therapy.

There's one guy who doesn't speak English, he just speaks Polish. He has burns almost all over his body. How do you provide for such an array of disabilities? So, in that sense, I can bemoan the fact that they don't provide for me, but on the other hand, I can take a step back and appreciate that, at the level of their thinking, what are they going to do? Provide a Polish interpreter for the Polish guy, and buttons I can handle, and things that this extremely diverse group of injured, diseased and disabled people need? Now, I would think that there might be certain things they can do which would cut across all of these kinds of things.

Jay: Yeah, that's what I was going to say. I think there are categories of response they could make to the particular needs of people without it being too costly. I have a hunch that as a result of this experience you are going to try to sort out those categories and help an institution like this look at innovations to assist patient recovery, the lack of which might have more to do with resistance to change than technology or cost.

Frank: Well, a case in point is that no one talked to me about what I did, what I'd like to do, and what I could continue doing here. No one came and said, 'Okay, well, how do you spend your day here? What times of the day would you like someone to come in and set up a tape recorder? What parts of the day do you need someone to come in who is not a nurse or a therapist?' The recreational therapists—who are concerned with your recreation, your avocation, your hobbies—simply try to design things like bingo games, social clubs, or cooking clubs that have a very narrow usefulness for a small group of patients. As I walk through the halls I see that many patients spend hours and hours each day staring at the wall. That's what I did and I still have to do it. I'm caught; I'm stuck—staring-at-the-wall-syndrome.

Jay: There is the part of you that stares at the walls, but there's also the part of you that walks the halls. That's the part that is already the observer, the investigator.

Frank: Yeah, I've been aware of that, because not only do I observe them but I observe myself.

I foresee the time when if I've made great effort and gotten someone from someplace and said, 'set up the tape recorder', I could start dictating or I could listen to a book or something. So far, the most I've been capable of doing is getting a switch for my radio. Sometimes I've just sat here and listened to music. Only recently, when [my son] Dylan was here, was I able to set up the talking book, Ishmael, and now I'm well into that. Vic Kestenbaum [colleague and friend] has in mind my listening to old radio shows: "Amos and Andy", "The Lone Ranger" or "The Shadow", and those programs are sometimes broadcast by WGBH. The idea is that they are thoroughly relaxing, totally simplistic. They are an entertaining way of passing time. Cousins (Norman Cousins, An Anatomy of an Illness) talks about humor and illness, and how when he got sick he wanted to get as many Marx Brothers films as he could because he wanted to laugh, because he felt that that was a way of dealing with sickness. Another way is to keep your mind occupied, to keep entertained, and become interested in what the next chapter says, or the next radio program. One of the things about reading a book is you are always looking forward to what's happening next. (laughs) And you do that in your life, but you also do that when you read a Tolstoy novel; you get hooked into it and you get totally immersed in the characters and the action. When you put it down and go away, you are wondering what's going to come next.

There is something about this place which is one day at a time; what's going to come next is the same thing that came the day before. That other part—the recreational part—exists in a simplistic form, but not in ways in which I think might really change the atmosphere of the place.

Jay: As I think about your research interests, they have a lot to do with how schools and other institutions respond or don't respond to the experience of the teacher, the child, whoever it is. Here you are, right smack in the middle of all this. Part of each day, depending on your mood and so forth, should be devoted to this generative investigation: a patient-scholar or a scholar-patient, whatever the equivalent is to the participant-observer. You take to this stuff. I think it's your life blood, part of your recovery. It's part of your mission, part of what you have to offer untold numbers of other patients who are in places like this. As I listen to you, I feel the vitality of that.

Frank: One subject would be the buoyancy of most of the nursing staff, their humor. There are a few exceptions of people who are moody; you expect people to have good moods and bad moods. But it seems to me there are an awful lot of nurses every day I've been here who have been buoyant, intrigued by any changes that took place in my body, my daily developments. They've always been on the bright side of things, and that's interesting. It's like a really good actor who, no matter what is happening, can play that role. There are nurses—no matter what's happening in their lives, they come here and smile, and they are working with this conglomeration of people of different ages, different problems. People with burns, people with huge sores that won't close up, and people who are, on the surface, very unattractive or difficult to look at. Yet the nurses blow in and have this buoyancy. There are only two nurses I have seen who don't look at anyone and are very officious, so that's quite a percentage.

Jay: Your research could be an exhaustive description of all the different parties, the visitors, the nurses, the doctors, the therapists. If you think of it in terms of a novel by Tolstoy, you think of all the different characters, they are all here.

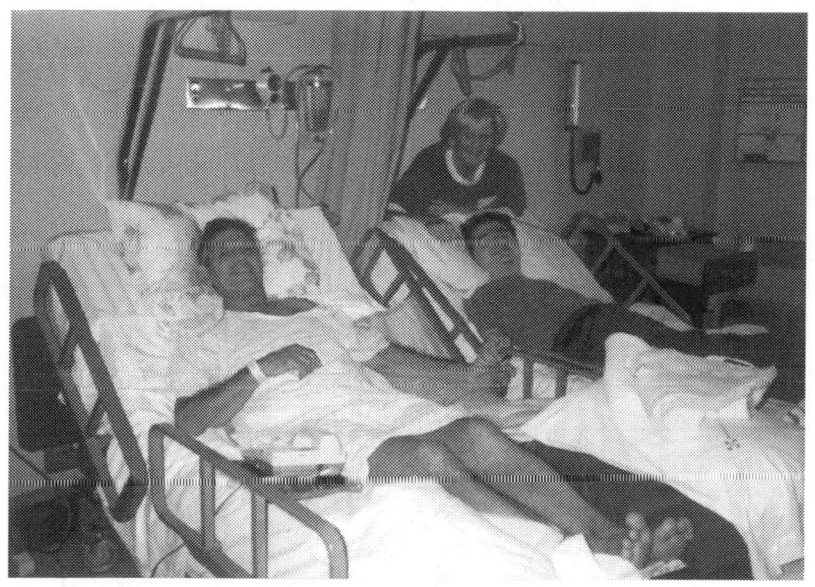

Frank at Rehab Hospital, Boston, MA 1992

AURA'S PERSPECTIVE: HOSPITALIZATION

I am a Buddhist, an agnostic one, not sure if there's a god or an afterlife. And yet, eight years after Frank's death, I write thinking he might read this – fearing that he'll know what I was experiencing during the last six years of his life and indeed, even during his after-life: how hopeful I was, when he began to wiggle his toes, use the razor, and climb stairs, that everything would go back to the way it had been; how careful I was to drive ever so cautiously, fearful that something might happen to me and that he'd have to go to a nursing home; how resentful that our relationship changed after his accident and I could no longer share the inane happenings of the day because, try as he did, he could no longer hear them; how angry that he didn't acknowledge how hard it was for me, even though I knew he knew and that he cared – it was just too difficult for him to do so without also feeling responsible for it; how mixed my feelings were after he died, my life no longer circumscribed and encumbered by his disability. But I am also hopeful that he'll know what I'm feeling now: how sad I am that he's not been around to see our children become the exceptional people they are; how lovely my memories of his exuberance and fearlessness; how protected I felt; how lonely I feel now. To have his love again, his companionship, how sweet that would be.

What did happen that drowsy August afternoon in 1992 to change our lives, to alter so profoundly who we were? Frank had been playing squash; he did everything with a zest that left younger men reeling. He'd been in a game at the 'Y' with Spike, one of his squash buddies, when he decided to run after a ball that most would have left for lost. He hit his head against the wall and suffered an incomplete spinal cord injury; a contusion of the spine. Although his spine had not been severed, the severe contusion meant that for years after he would suffer the most excruciating nerve pain. His nervous system would play cruel jokes on him, sending him false messages that he was burning up or freezing. His accident rendered him quadriplegic. Although he had some gross motor abilities, in both his hands and legs, he would never walk independently again. Despite the pain and permanent paralysis, Frank never lost his humor, often claiming victory in the very game that was his undoing.

August 27th, my sister's birthday: Spike called at work and told me that Frank had had an accident. He was okay but had been taken to the emergency at the Brigham Hospital; he couldn't move, had lost sensation in his legs. I was a staff attorney for the Massachusetts Department of Social Services. My supervisor told me to leave as soon as I could. She'd assign my cases to another attorney until I was able to come back. I was bewildered and mechanically did as she said. By the time I arrived at the hospital, Frank seemed in good spirits although clearly scared. He'd always bounced back from his injuries and mishaps and we both had faith that this time would be no different. We volleyed back and forth, like his near-miss squash ball, between black humor, fear, and hope.

I was asked to wait in the waiting room while they administered swelling-reducing steroids to him. After a while a doctor came out and told me that Frank's accident was serious; that they had put him on medication to reduce swelling – something that had to be done within the first eight hours after such a catastrophic injury. They had done everything right, but he might not recover movement; he might never walk again. The words were like continuing after-shocks to my flailing system. How could he be saying those things to me? Why couldn't they just fix whatever was wrong? The one person I would have turned to for comfort and support was in a recovery room experiencing his own purgatory.

Miraculously, my friend Nancy O'Malley walked into the waiting room. I never even asked her how she'd heard about Frank so thankful was I to see her. I drove home late that night through the Callahan Tunnel, my thoughts and emotions screeching and colliding like bumper cars at an amusement park. For a horrifying moment I glimpsed the future: dark matter, escapeless emptiness. I cried out, but there was only myself to calm me down and ensure that I made it home safely.

The second night after the accident, Frank called for a nurse to help him scratch an itchy eye – an eye that was now off-limits to his once-deft fingers. A Russian male nurse, who came to his call, misunderstood Frank and scratched his ear instead. Frank became hysterical and the nursing staff tied his arm, the only limb he was barely able to control, to the bed. In the morning, when I came in, I had my own tantrum, incensed at what I perceived as a cruel act.

After a week at the Brigham, Frank and I were asked to decide which chronic care hospital he would be transferred to. He'd have to be out by the end of the week. Facing his imminent discharge, in a state of bewilderment and shock, I began a frenzied search for a rehab hospital. It was a cool, rainy day when a colleague and friend of Frank's accompanied me on visits to a handful of hospitals in the Greater Boston area. I felt clueless, my ability to think clearly compromised, so I was grateful for her support. I chose a rehab center that seemed more cheerful than the others - cheerful was important, anything to counteract the gloom that had settled over Frank and me. The center also had a good reputation in the Greater Boston area, took spinal cord-injured patients and was relatively close to where we lived in Winthrop.

Frank and I arrived at his new room – new bed, new world, on the Saturday of Labor Day weekend 1992. The hospital was short of staff, it being a long holiday weekend. We still had hopes that his paralysis was only temporary. I sat on his bed, holding his barely sensate hand; his fingers were clammy and refused to unfurl. I could not utter words of reassurance - Frank would know they'd be empty. I could sit with him and crack small jokes about the place, the people, the situation. The room itself was bright with the usual trappings of a hospital room. There were two televisions jutting from the top of the wall and a small bathroom to be shared by the two occupants of the room. We laughed and cried.

His roommate was a young man from Bosnia. He was in much worse shape than Frank. After a diving accident had left him paraplegic, he'd had surgery in Bosnia that had gone terribly awry and now he was totally quadriplegic. He had to be hoisted in and out of bed with a complex contraption whose technical name escapes me. Several days later, when Frank, experiencing a Eureka moment, elatedly announced he could wiggle his toes, his roommate cried, not out of resentment, but out of happiness for Frank. He knew what euphoria it must be to wiggle your toes. Another man in Frank's wing had had severe burns over most of his body. He had no family in the US and only spoke Polish. It was heart-wrenching. Frank asked a friend of ours who was born in Poland, if she'd come and talk to him, just so he could hear someone he could understand.

The early days were busy, with doctors, therapists and visitors coming each day. The hospital was clearly short of staff and Frank's needs were huge. I took a formal leave-of-absence from work and put everything else on hold. All else that was going on at home or with my children is a big blur. Seth, who was nineteen, had moved out west to work on a cattle ranch in Nevada. Anelisa, then seventeen, was getting ready to start college at Boston University. And Dylan, age twenty-three, had been working on a tree farm for troubled kids in Vermont. After the accident, Dylan left his job and moved back home to help out.

ACCIDENT - JAY

The accident
came from nowhere,
predators' lair

yet looking back,
event and man
seemed
each other's match,

but they were different
injury,
accident's offspring,
refused to yield

altered,
Frank accommodated
and was transformed,
becoming more himself

in rough marriage
they stayed together
for six years;
fierce injury,
restrictions

scrawled
in pain;
wild man
spinning his wheelchair
in the snow
or, tipped over,
waiting,
while Truman barked
for help

The Marriage Vows - Aura

Twenty two summers ago I *took you*
to be my wedded husband
to have and to hold,
to love and to cherish.

Then, on a drowsy day
when time danced a waltz
in the weary arms of August
and overheated blossoms drooped
like bowed heads at Sunday mass,
Spike called –
the ambulance came.

Now, you lie tormented
by stilled limbs
while I linger
by your bedside
with stunned tongue.
.

I'll stay the night, nights -
sleep on a roll-away
wait until your frightened eyes can sleep
hold your spastic hand in mine -
in sickness or in health .

FRANK AND JAY, SATURDAY, OCTOBER 3, 1992: "SO I DIDN'T HAVE MUCH CONTROL OVER EVERYTHING, BUT IN A WAY I DID."

Frank: Faucets and urination seem to be working very effectively. (chuckles) I seem to be making great inroads on my incontinency. Really interesting events at my physical therapy session today, which started out rather disastrously. My chair was rolled up with the controls side closest to the mat, which I objected to, but which I finally agreed to because the therapist wanted my right hand on the mat. But when she took the arm of the chair with the control, she accidentally hit the recline lever, at which point I shot backwards in the chair.

Jay: The chair just opened up?

Frank: The chair opened up and I ended up in a supine position. I thought I was going to go flying off the chair or it was going to tip over. I became quite hysterical, and my sister and brother-in-law were watching all this, and the therapist was totally confused because she didn't know how that chair operated. And she couldn't find the switch! She didn't even know there was a switch! (laughter) She reassured me it would not go down any further, and I was able to explain where the switch was. She finally found it and I told her how to press the lever so that I went back up. At which point I was totally out of control, afraid, very vulnerable. And then she cradled me and assured me things were

21

okay. Assured me that there had been no danger at any point in time! (laughs)

Jay: As her teeth chattered! (laughs)

Frank: She became noticeably unnerved and I reassured her that I was okay! (laughter)

Jay: You take good care of the staff!

Frank: You know, we talked and reassured each other. Finally I said I was ready for action, so then she proceeded to get me on the mat and practice my sitting up, which certainly is one of the most taxing, one of the most difficult, demanding things I do. One of the most threatening things to me of my whole recovery is the fact that I seem to have no balance.

Jay: So you feel at any moment you can tip over?

Frank: Right, right, no control. If I'm going forward I can't correct to go back. I feel that I could even just tilt over, like an inanimate object.

Jay: Even if you had not been bedridden for as long as you have and had full control of your muscles, I'm sure you'd still have a real sensation the first time you sat up.

Frank: No, this is much more than that, this is total loss. When I first started this balancing therapy, no more than three weeks ago, I didn't even know where my balance point was. Not only couldn't I do it, I would say, "Is it here?" and she would say, "No", so she would shift me around. First I had to have some realization of where it was; it took a week just to have that realization. Then I was able to sit up for fifteen to twenty seconds but with people all around me, in front of me, in back of me; and then I kind of made a breakthrough and was able to stay up for a minute or two. A day or two would go by between each session.

Last Thursday, when Aura was there with two students, I had several trials where I felt a lot more confidence but I was still a little shaky. Then I stayed up for more than six minutes and that included talking to them and looking around, telling a joke, laughing. That was monumental. Then on Friday I did the tilt board and went up to almost ninety degrees, much better than I had done before, without my blood pressure crashing and without getting terrified. And it is a little terrifying to get up on that board.

After the incident today where I inadvertently reclined, fell apart and was comforted by the therapist and wound up comforting her, she sat me up in the balancing position and simply told me to put my hands on my lap. I said, "I can't do that, I need them at my side". She said, "Well, I don't know." She was a new therapist, someone who I had never had before. So I had my feet on the board, on the little box that was in front of me and I put my hands on my lap, and lo and behold I sat up! I couldn't quite believe it but I did it. Not only that but some of the giddiness of Thursday had gone and I had a lot more confidence.

Jay: Maybe the traumatic incident took the panic out of the situation; there wasn't any left

Frank: The other thing it might be related to is that I'd been on my stomach several times for the first time before that day and the night before. The effect of being on my stomach meant that my hip inflexion was straightening out and that will certainly affect balance. At any rate, I was able to do that.

Then she proceeded to tell me that she was going to pull the box away from my feet. I objected to that and said I wasn't ready for that, but she encouraged me to try and I said okay. So then I just sat there balanced, with her a good three feet away. Not needing the people all around me. Talking to my sister and jesting about it. That was an exciting event. Seems to confirm what this doctor had said the day before, that I was ready to move on. And that's why he recommended me going on my stomach. That was a necessary phase which would end up in me walking. He couldn't say when that would happen: in a week, ten days, two weeks or a month.

Jay: But his optimism and long-term view puts the thing in a somewhat different context for you.

Frank: Oh yeah, I'm sure that affected it. Maybe the traumatic incident affected it. Maybe I developed a few more neural connections.

There have been a lot of positive things that have happened with friends. Also, I had gone to this School of Education reception the night before. We went out about six o'clock in a chair car; I was wearing a new shirt that Aura had bought me. New sweater, new sweats and being all dressed up and hair combed to Aura's satisfaction—not to mine but to hers! Spent two enjoyable hours with colleagues from BU [Boston University].

Jay: Was most of the faculty there?

Frank: Well, I'd say about half of the faculty, a lot of the people who had visited me in the hospital. So I'm sure that had an effect on me. Everyone was telling me how wonderfully I was doing. Sounded somewhat tortured, but I mean for a lot of them it was true.

Jay: Some of them haven't seen you for a while and probably hadn't —

Frank: But I was in a festive mood. I was joking. I think that had a great effect on me. In fact, one faculty member had told me his brother couldn't walk and was in a wheel chair, I don't know the circumstances. He said, "The two of you are going in the opposite direction. You keep on laughing and thinking about improvement and getting out and seeing people. People who visit you in the hospital come back and say they enjoyed the visit." He said that when they visited his brother, it was painful and depressing and that he didn't have any outlook. Maybe that's due to the fact that I have some rightful optimism and he has some rightful pessimism.

Jay: Or that the whole system can become self-defeating very easily. You really had to fight. If this fellow's brother encountered the kind of milieu that you did at the Brigham Hospital and its set-up, it would be very easy to become discouraged.

Frank: That experience was terrible, but it wasn't because they were terrible people. It was simply because my fate was so indeterminate. I didn't know what was going to happen. I had visions of my being a quadriplegic, not having hands or feet, for the rest of my life. Yet it was clear that I was thinking. [Here, at the rehab hospital] A lot of people came to visit me, there were always hoards of people here, and I could always talk to them and joke with them. I remember the big moment was when I could wiggle my toes. I look back on that now as a great event. In fact I remember saying to the dean when he visited me, "I wiggled my toes. Do you think that's worth a publication?"

Even though I had no control over switches or lights or turning myself over in bed or brushing my teeth or eating or scratching, one of the early things I remember is that I began to get some movement in my right arm. Whenever I got it up to a certain point and put it over my head, it would fall on my face. With full weight it would smash my nose or my eye. I remember [my son] Seth thought that was very funny. It was kind of funny even though it kind of hurt. So I appreciated the humor and sometimes I did it just simply because it was funny.

So I didn't have much control over everything, but in a way I did. I guess I controlled the atmosphere—whether it was going to be humorous or friendly or warm or deadly; whether people would visit and never come back. Or whether people would come and keep on coming back, because the only reason people come back is they enjoy being here. I figured they wouldn't come back just because they felt sorry for me. I didn't do this as a manipulation thing. I didn't say to myself, 'I'm going to entertain Jay Clark and then he'll come back'. But, in effect, that's what I did and some of them told me that. Some people told me, "Well I'm coming back because I get so much out of it." (laughter)

Jay: That can mean a lot of different things! (laughs)

Frank: I was convinced, and not disappointed at the idea, that after a week or two in rehab, I would only see my family and a few close friends. And I do see my family and a few close friends, but at least ten or fifteen faculty have kept on coming and they are not my intimate friends. They're becoming my intimate friends (laughs) because of their coming back, because of their affection. I don't know. It's been very amazing in many ways, and a somewhat miraculous experience to see that.

Jay: One of the first things you said to me when I called you on the phone, after you'd been here for a couple of days, was that the injury had changed your whole life and attitude. What you are describing is its changing of your friendships and relationships with these faculty members. It's a powerful thing when you make a change like that.

Frank: And that's why it was so important that I went to that reception on Friday night. They saw me wheeling around and joking. They had a chance to say something and ... well, a lot has happened, apparently, in the school too. So that is interesting, the extent to which I controlled some very important things about what happened. And I know it started at the Brigham.

Jay: So people started almost from—not the first day obviously—but after that, people began coming.

Frank: Oh, yeah. My sister and Aura's sister came down and people from other states and around here, Winthrop and everything. I guess what this conversation leads me to dwell on, which I hadn't dwelt on before, is the extent to which I was in control, although I continually felt I was out of control, just as I did when that recliner went on. Another time a nurse kind of dropped me and I started to fall out of the bed and I got hysterical; that was probably inside of my first week, here. Another time, someone picked me up by my armpits and I hadn't realized it, but no one can pick me up by my armpits; it just destroys me. Oh yeah, there was another time when it looked like I was falling and someone caught me. And I had the same overwhelming loss. It kind of attacked my integrity and my person.

Jay: At that point you're kind of poised in a life and death situation. Given the injury, it could be an extremely serious thing if someone mishandled you.

Frank: And they are bound to. I'm heavy. I'm helpless. They are trying. There are distractions. There have been other times when I've been transferred and I've ended up on the very edge of the thing and … of course now I shout out much more readily and I'm much more demanding of how people treat me and how they handle me.

So, it's total lack of control, total physical vulnerability, alongside this control (laughs) of the psychological and the social environment.

Jay: But while no one can handle that perfectly, you have some capacity to— not accept, but live with that, in a way a lot of people may not.

Frank: Apparently!! (laughs heartily) Apparently I've been buoyant enough to, although I've fallen apart a number of times. There have been nights when I was in great pain. But I think I've always been able to laugh a little about something.

Jay: I guess it's laugh or croak! (laughter)

Frank: And then the nurse, [getting ready to transfer me from the bed to the chair], when I said "Oh, God! Watch out! Watch out!" she says, "Don't worry. I'm not going to drop you, its too much damn paperwork!!" (laughter) Another time a nurse said, "This is the first time I've ever done this!" (laughter)

Jay: Just what you wanted to hear! (laughter) At least she was honest! (laughter)

Frank: Every morning, my routine is that after I get up they give me a suppository to have regular bowel movements. Then they put me on a bed pan. They get me out of bed and put me on a commode and wheel me into the bathroom. So today, there I was, sitting on the toilet, and Aura was there and there were three other nurses, and we were having; a conversation! (laughs heartily) Just like we were out in the kitchen!

Jay: Louis XIV! (laughter)

Frank: And we were talking and joking and everything. (laughs heartily)

Jay: A real adaptation! (laughter)

Frank: You don't exactly think of it that way. (laughter)

Jay: The only thing is that, when you get back to normal and invite everyone in while you take a shit they're going to get a little upset! (extended laughter) The trouble is, unless there's five people in the bathroom with you, you can't take a shit! (extended laughter) You'll have to enlarge the bathroom!

Frank: Maybe this chronicle is one of humor and pain and pain and humor. And the pain becomes bearable because of the humor. I have no doubt about that. I don't know if it's (Norman) Cousins' theme or a variation of his theme, but it constantly comes up.

Jay: Well, there's an underlying irony to the whole thing. You're a connoisseur of the ironic anyway.

Frank: (laughing) if I wasn't?

Jay: You're going to be when you get through it!

Frank: As we talk and as I laugh, I've got these huge muscle belts: one right here across my chest and another right here across my stomach. And the more I laugh, the more it hurts! (laughs) And the more they tighten up, it's like someone's got some kind of a—what do they call it—like a lever or something that tightens up and tightens up.

Jay: Does it stay? Is it there now?

Frank: Yeah.

Jay: Well then, just for a moment, concentrate on your breathing and be aware of the out breath. Touch your breath on its way and feel it dissolve in front of you. Feel the air coming out of your mouth and nose.

Frank: Well, I have to change my position a little bit. What's happened is that I have a lot of weight on this left shoulder. The left shoulder is the weak shoulder.

Jay: Okay, so maybe I need to—

Frank: First take the pillow out from between my legs—

Jay: While we do that maybe I'll turn the tape off or do you want a live recording of how this happens?

Frank: Okay, a live recording. Why don't you pull this pillow out from under my right shoulder. Okay. Now that takes the pressure off the left shoulder. And maybe you could pull the sheet over and get me centered. .. Good.

Jay: Okay. One, two—how's that?

Frank: Good.

Jay: I'll turn this tape off while we work on the relaxing. ... (break in recording while Frank dissipated some of the tension in his body)

★ ★ ★

Frank: As I think of the different people I interact with, some of them just don't have a sense of humor. With some the relationship is okay. My primary nurse has no sense of humor. But I have another nurse, Mary, an Irish woman, who has an incredible sense of humor, many of them do. They joke about things. They joke about me. I joke about them. I laugh at things sometimes when I am in pain. Sometimes I cry when I do things that are really...I know that I cried after I was able to sit up without using my feet and without hands.

THE ACCIDENT AND THE MAN

On the day of Frank's accident I was driving west across Idaho with my wife Kitty and our son David, headed to Burns, Oregon. By the evening of the next day we would arrive in Bend to stay overnight before pressing on to Portland, where we would leave David, who was taking a year off from college, working in order to travel with his girlfriend during the following spring. We were to pick up Kitty's sister in Portland for the return drive across the country. The news of the accident would not reach me for another twelve days. We arrived at our home near Boston to find a note saying that Frank had sustained a serious injury while playing squash. The news didn't sink in, even though I paused over the word 'serious'.

I regarded Frank as indestructible, adept at courting and escaping from perilous situations. Over the twenty-five years I had known him, he had sustained a number of injuries playing squash and tennis, some requiring him to wear a sling for a few days. But, with the exception of a wrenched back—suffered twelve years earlier in a tennis match with me—that sidelined him for several months, Frank had never incurred a major injury. Surely his resilience would assure a speedy recovery.

After I had spoken with Aura I began to realize that this time Frank's prognosis was uncertain. Following his initial hospitalization, he had been transferred to a rehabilitation hospital. This injury was more grave than any he had sustained in the past.

Frank's career had involved teaching, evaluating, and advocating for the handicapped, and preparing graduate students for professional work in the field of special education. His outgoing personality, his love of adventure and his critical and comprehensive view of institutions serving handicapped children made him a formidable advocate for those whose condition prevented them from speaking out in their own behalf. On numerous occasions Frank's service as an expert witness in legal cases around the country had led to the modification of institutional policies and procedures. It was thus profoundly ironic that a champion of those at the bottom of the ladder of physical self-reliance should find himself at the mercy of professionals who failed to treat him as an equal and sometimes perceived his critical voice as manifesting a lack of commitment or cooperation.

Frank contended not only with the hospital staff but also with a shattered nervous system and muscles no longer responsive to his will. Now a quadriplegic, he required the help of his physical therapists to determine the position of his limbs and the degree to which his body was balanced when he attempted to sit, stand or walk. He descended into a realm where he had to deal with his body as if it were a foreign object or, as he put it, a puppet, the parts of which he attempted to control with strings. With many therapists and nurses, Frank developed relationships of an order of intimacy reflecting the fact that they, in effect, became part of his body, filling in for damaged neurons and disabled limbs.

During Frank's second week at the hospital, he made a request of me. "I want to document what I see going on in the hospital and what's happening to me as a patient. Since I can't write, I'd like to talk with you. A lot happens each day, inside my body and in my exchanges with staff and with other patients. I think our talking would help me deepen my understanding of my injury, the hospital and the whole process of my rehabilitation." I quickly agreed, considering it an honor that he wanted to explore his hospital experience with me. I believed that Frank hoped that after his recovery he would be able to use transcripts of these conversations to portray the challenges that patients could encounter. As he spoke of the accomplishments and frustrations of each day I was struck with the intensity of the feelings he disclosed. I soon realized that a regular opportunity to reflect might help him maintain sanity in the face of constant struggle and crisis.

Frank had always pressed his students to evaluate critically the data they collected in their research. Now he would, himself, use our conversations to record and reflect upon the torrent of events that descended upon him during his hospital stay and afterward, when he returned home late in November of 1992.

As events unfolded, Frank was not able to use the transcripts of the eighteen conversations that occurred between September 30 and December 28 of 1992. Overwhelming and nearly constant pain closed in upon him for the following four-and-a-half years, ending our recordings, though we continued to talk. He never reviewed what he might have referred to with a wry smile as his own experience of "participant observation", the method of clinical research that he often encouraged his students to pursue when investigating how institutions deal with the handicapped.

* * *

When Frank hired me in 1967, out of graduate school, to teach in the Department of Special Education at Boston University, his vigor and competence offered a model for living I had not encountered in university life. My instructors kept their distance or, in cases where I got to know them, seemed so engrossed in academic pursuits that I imagined the rest of their lives as impoverished. During my first year at BU, I realized I was teaching with someone as deeply interested in his world outside the university as he was in studying the needs of the handicapped and the institutions attempting to meet those needs. I learned that he was devoted to

Max, his seven-year old son from a previous marriage, relished tennis, squash and novels; that he rode a motorcycle, sailed his boat around the islands in Boston Harbor and played the banjo. I also discovered that he was skilled in carpentry and loved to go bird-watching in wildlife areas along the coast.

A friendship of twenty-five years and close collegial relationship from 1967 until 1981, when I left BU to direct a clinic in Boston, led me to regard Frank as a mentor. At the time of the accident, I dismissed whatever might have happened to him as something that could not alter his personality or role in my life. Looking back now, fifteen years after his injury, and ten years after his death, I see that while it brought about catastrophic changes in Frank's life, he emerged more deeply aware of himself and his relationships with others: friends, hospital staff members and family. Those changes also precipitated a bonding between us that made the next six years the most intimate period of our friendship.

Originality characterized Frank's professional and personal style. He encouraged many of his graduate students to employ participant observation, a dynamic and complex method, in studying institutions' treatment of children with special needs. Instead of using a formal means for collecting information, such as a questionnaire or checklist of anticipated behaviors, participant observers open themselves to whatever happens as a result of immersion in the setting they are studying. They are not in total control of the data that is generated. This courtship of the unanticipated may produce richer information than would a position of scientific neutrality, but it also requires more flexibility, both as observer and in the analysis of the information collected. Participant observers function on the interface between detachment and objectivity on one hand and intense engagement with the observed on the other.

One of the most popular members of the School of Education Faculty, Frank was also one of the most controversial. He was a free spirit, comfortable in confrontations with others. "Even if you loved Frank, you hated him," said one member of another department whose policies he had often criticized at faculty meetings. In our own department, it seemed to me that some people tried to stay out of his way while others—more apt to become close friends—fought back. "Oh, Frank, fuck off!" exclaimed one woman in response to his sarcastic comment at a faculty meeting; decades later, she was to visit him regularly at the rehab hospital.

Though self disciplined—he arranged the tools in his basement so carefully that he could unfailingly tell an aide searching for an implement the exact place on the wall where it could be found—Frank savored the unexpected. Much of the adventure in his life came from plunging into things, assuming that he would deal with whatever might result. And deal he did, for he was quick of mind and reflex. He held a greater advantage over me on the squash court than he did in tennis because squash requires split-second reflexes, whereas tennis allowed me a little more time to respond. He could improvise easily, seeing the outlines of a dining room table in a piece of driftwood or a manifestation of instructional style in a teacher's response to a sudden classroom occurrence.

By its nature, Frank's injury—a contusion of the spinal cord—was unusual and obscure. A complete severance of the spinal column leads to a predictable and relatively static loss of function, according to the location of the fracture; the prognosis of a contusion is more difficult to ascertain. Uncertainty about treatment and recovery dominated Frank's life, from the moment the specialist at the Brigham told him it would take months to determine how much of his functioning he would regain.

Frank's characteristic willingness to take a risk and his ability to engage with its consequences were intrinsic to his response to his injury. He didn't invite his accident, but a lifestyle which tended to generate the unforeseen may have eased his entry into an altered existence, transferring his professional focus from classrooms serving children with special needs to the corridors, nurses' stations and physical therapy rooms of his hospital. He spoke of encounters with other patients and his sense that feelings of isolation and despair might influence their recovery more profoundly than their treatment plan. Frank created, through his injury, an opportunity to study yet another institution committed to assisting the handicapped.

RENEWED CONVERSATION - JAY

In times past
our lives
informed our talks
classes we taught,
faculty meetings,
squash or tennis tilts,
departmental crises

now we met
to speak of injury,
pain, ambition, triumph
insights
outrage with institutional attempts
to pack him in its suitcase

he led,
I followed
a role not new to me
as I look in upon
the worlds of clients

but this was different,
our talks poised
between exchange

of friendship
and of therapy
speaking, the only mode
accessible to him
to let his trials be known

recorded,
he hoped our conversations would inform
a study of another kind
of personal journey
amidst institutional confines

so we embarked
on dialogue
at once
familiar and new

Part II. STARTING OVER

Frank and Jay discuss the issue of disability and integrity: what is the essence of wholeness? Frank is struck with the irony of some friends expecting miraculous recovery because of his strength, juxtaposed with the view of others that some day he will be whole again, but not for now, it is implied, the integrity of his personhood had been compromised.

Frank speaks of the tremendous task of trying to attend to and coordinate all the necessary movements in order to walk, recalling the fable of the Centipede who, after trying to describe how he was able to move forward, never walked again. He begins to feel "silenced and extinguished" by his nurse and reflects on the profound changes within himself brought about by the experience of being a patient.

AURA'S PERSPECTIVE: FAMILY & FRIENDS

At the rehab hospital, family, friends and students from Boston University visited Frank's room on a daily basis. Despite the hospital's good reputation, we soon became painfully aware that many of Frank's physical or psychological needs could not adequately be met. He was often left in the grips of unbearable pain, especially at night. Because of this, I began to stay over in his room so that at least I could help turn him when the inexplicable neuropathic pains got the best of him.

Frank had an incomplete spinal cord injury; the cord was not completely severed. The good news was that eventually he would be able to stand up, with lots of help, and to walk with a built-up walker. The bad news was that the pain that surged through his body like electric shocks, making him feel as if his chest were being squeezed with steel belts, was excruciating and intractable. Sometimes he could find relief if he were turned over, or massaged, or sat up. Sometimes it helped to have his legs raised or his fingers stretched.

During the day, he often had visitors, giving me time to go home and sleep or tend to household chores that were piling up. The day was gratifying for Frank, with family, friends, students and colleagues visiting and assisting him. As a professor of special education, Frank had spent decades teaching students about the needs and the rights of disabled children. Now some of his students helped with the mechanical stuff, trying to figure out how he might be able to answer the phone or press the call button for the nurse. When Frank returned home, they rigged up the house so that he could put his lamp on by himself, hold a cup of water, answer the phone. The husband of one of his students spent hours installing a voice activated word processing program. Others rigged up ways he could press the buttons of a tape recorder.

Frank and I were amazed and awed by the visitors who came during those early rehab months. Their generosity and good wishes kept us from sinking into a quicksand of despair. But there were also times when we were stunned by visitors who clearly expected Frank to be heroic, to have a "stiff upper lip," to be resolute, stalwart, brave. "Frank's a fighter, he'll get through this" ; "You gotta keep a sense of humor and you can't give up"; "He's tough – he'll survive" - statements intended to be comforting instead left a sour, disconcerting taste. Frank saw them as part of the Christopher Reeve or the Hollywood need-to-heroify-life syndrome: he shall walk no matter what. Those who crumble, give in, are suicidal, or just get by, are not worthy of exaltation in a screenplay or in life.

Other visitors would assure Frank that some day he'd be "whole" again. This was even more objectionable. He once said, "I think that's a common way of viewing it. People are invalid, in–valid, not whole. You're not intact if you're missing a leg, or in my case whatever I am. That's a problem, the way people view disability: a real threat to someone's integrity." As if any of us are truly 'whole'.

Frank continued teaching and advising his students throughout all the nightmarish weeks and months that followed his injury, and for that matter, right up until he died. Teaching was perhaps the most potent medicine he could have. For me, the initial shock and grief led to wanting to do all in my power to ensure his care, even if that meant quitting my job and sleeping in a tiny roll-out bed in the cramped semi-private hospital room. Others were quicker than I to see the sheer exhaustion and ill health that were afflicting me during those early months. My world had come to a standstill; all that mattered was a need to assuage Frank's suffering. I was lucky my children were young adults and often wondered how I would have fared if they had been younger and I had had to attend to them as well.

A reversal of roles began almost immediately. I found myself having to be the strong one, having to be the advocate. It was especially heartbreaking to see how much Frank, who had been such a fighter and would stand up to the most intimidating of people, now needed to rely on me to make his case at the hospital. He was demoralized, in unremitting pain, and confused, unsure of what functioning if any, he would recover. I learned quickly how to help him stand; how to roll him on his side in order to make the bed and how to slide him to a wheel chair. I would demand that he be cared for appropriately, and if it didn't happen, I would do it myself, taking him for showers, helping him eat and getting him dressed. On a more mundane level, he had always been the one to pay the bills and keep tabs on our finances. This too would change. There were times when I felt I was drowning in chores, all the old ones as well as the new ones generated by Frank's needs. It would take a long time to arrive at a place where we would achieve balance in our life again.

At the hospital, our friend Jay Clark offered to take over my vigil one night a week. It was in this way that he and Frank decided to record conversations about the goings-on of the day. Frank was an academic, social scientist, activist and advocate. Taping his impressions of his strange new state of being during those critical months in rehab made sense given who he was, and yet I don't think his desire to tape these conversations was driven primarily by an intellectual or academic need. Rather, it was driven by a need to assert authority over that part of his life that he still had control over, his mind. After all, his intellect and perspicacity were every bit as sharp after the accident as before. Like a traveler in a foreign land, he was keenly aware and in awe of the new landmarks that surrounded him. He was Gulliver in a hospital bed. Through the tapes, his mind could travel through the Lilliputian or Houyhnhnm lands of his predicament. He was in his element, doing what he did best, observing the environment, human interactions and above all, himself. He would reflect, weigh, ponder, critique, assess, laugh, hope, philosophize, love, hate, cry, fall asleep, worry about the toll his injury was taking on me and the kids, enlist Jay's help in repositioning him, hallucinate, and reminisce. He would voice fears of never walking again, hopes of someday walking, and joy at having taken a few steps. Quadriplegia had effectively subjugated his body, even his spirits, but it would never subjugate his mind.

In October, with Frank still at the rehab hospital, our daughter Anelisa was scheduled for jaw surgery. Her jaw was not large enough to easily accommodate all of her teeth. She'd been waiting for this for years, as the surgery could not be performed until her bones had stopped growing. Finally, after emotionally and physically painful years of waiting, she was to have her operation at a most inopportune time - the start of her first semester at Boston University and in a period of major emotional trauma in her family's life. Nevertheless, she was not to be dissuaded. What a way to start college; what a way to start her young adult life. Her horoscope must have been horrified at the confluence of these events. She had her surgery at a hospital in Boston, not far from the rehab center. My sister Virginia came up from New York to sit and wait with me on the day of the operation. I didn't have to ask her; she knew I needed her to be with me. We brought books and magazines to the hospital waiting room, but all I could read were the glacier-like hands of the hospital clock. I had to keep reminding myself to breathe. When I was finally able to deliver the news to Frank that our daughter was well and in recovery we hugged and cried with relief. For Frank, who could not even be at the hospital with us, the ordeal had been enormous.

After the surgery, I divided my time between Anelisa, whose jaw would be wired shut for the next six weeks, and Frank, whose body was virtually wired shut, possibly forever. It was difficult to leave Frank when there was no one else around to help him. Any position he was in for too long would cause him great pain, and I didn't trust the nurses to be that attentive. At the same time, Anelisa was recuperating, stressed physically and mentally and in a situation where she couldn't communicate easily with any one. Once Anelisa came home, it was easier. Her friends were always around to bring her frappes, play cards with her, and just hang out and watch TV. When she felt up to it, she went to visit her father - a very emotional meeting. Her jaw was still wired shut and she became all choked up. Words would have been superfluous anyway.

FRANK AND JAY, TUESDAY, OCTOBER 6, 1992: "I DON'T THINK MY INTEGRITY WAS EVER COMPROMISED"

Frank: Someone visited me last night and said, "You know you're going to come together again." And I caught myself. I think that that is a common way of viewing it. People are invalid, in-valid. You're not valid, you're not whole, you are not intact if you are missing a leg or, in my case, whatever I am. I hadn't spoken to anyone about it. This woman said, in effect, "You're really coming together". So without trying to challenge her, I tried to explain how my own thinking had stumbled on this false perception. "That is a problem: people view disability as a real threat to someone's integrity." I tried to tell her, "I don't think my integrity was ever compromised in this whole thing and it still isn't." She became very defensive, "That's not what I meant."

Jay: The nature of being human is to be validated. If an experience is valid, it has integrity, even if there are disjunctive elements. Maybe people tend to think of an interruption of 'normal' experience of one's body or mind as not real or not whole—and that's not the case.

Frank: Or people who are blind or deaf. It applies to anyone who is 'incomplete'. In the spinal cord language, they use the terms 'complete' and 'incomplete': someone who is 'complete' has a complete injury and someone who is 'incomplete' has an

46

injury that is less than complete; that's almost the opposite of the lingo.

Jay: There is a latent assumption that a handicapped person's boundaries are not intact, a dangerous notion because it allows people to take advantage of others through control or pity. And it seems that this visitor came to a conclusion about you and the nature of your experience—

Frank: —which is, I claim, the prevailing view. I even thought that way about myself. But I caught myself, pretty quickly. At one point when Aura and I were talking shortly after the accident, I said, "Well, I have everything that is important." And we kind of talked about that. I could think and I could cry and I could laugh and I could interact with people. At the same time I couldn't walk and I couldn't use my hands. So, we just kind of marveled, or wondered about that.

Jay: The concept of wholeness gets into the existential realm. Are any of us whole? Against the background of "handicap" comes a concept of "wholeness" and against the background of official "wholeness" comes the question of whether, indeed, any of us are not broken in some way, incomplete or wounded. I was leading a support group this afternoon and one of the women in the group burst into tears because someone had said to her, "I don't know how you manage to do all that you do." That opened up something for her and she could get in touch with the pain of the intensity of all the work she was doing. Our logic or our physical sanity can delude us into thinking that we are completely whole, free of pain.

It strikes me that your encounter with all of this has had an almost shattering impact on a lot of people. I mean people that don't know you very well. I spoke with a friend last week and I shared with him what had gone on and he was just stunned. Maybe what society does with the injury is to turn its back on you and say that you're the person who is incomplete, when the fact is that something changes for other people.

Frank: And they reflect on the concept of their wholeness.

Jay: I think one of the profound effects of hearing about you or thinking about you has been to leave people with the sensation that they live on the edge. While you are having this physical sensation of lying on a concrete edge; I don't know if you still have it, but—

Frank: —I still have it—

Jay: —other people have that too, in a very different but similar kind of way.

You know, the one thing they have really done is they've got the TV at just the right angle for viewing.

Frank: Yeah, for this bed, I don't know whether so much for the other bed.

Jay: I think it's pretty well set up.

Nurse: (who has just entered) There's no sound.

Jay: A picture tells a thousand words. It's a pretty straightforward situation [baseball game is on], not much nuance to this game.

Frank: Do they play baseball in the Philippines?

Nurse: No, more basketball. (Nurse removes urinal)

Frank: (Looking at amount of urine in urinal) Oh, it's more than I thought it would be.

Nurse: 200 cc.

Frank: 200? Is that right? That's surprising. (Nurse cleans up) The powder might be in that box over there.

Nurse: Your bedsores are not as open as before.

Frank: I know. They don't bother me anymore.

Nurse: That's good, because before it was like an open sore, it's not anymore.

Frank: I'm not getting very wet anymore, this was the first time in three days.

Jay: It's been in the last week that you've been more keenly aware of wanting to pee and so forth.

Frank: Yes, that's made great strides lately.

Tape is turned off and another nurse has come in to prepare Frank for the night. It is after ten PM, most visitors have left and things are quieting down on the floor. After the nurse leaves, Frank reflects on what has happened since the last time he and Jay talked.

Frank: Just a little chronicle of things that have happened in the last couple of days: One of them comes under the category of almost mishap—well, there were two of them. I forget whether we spoke about the one where the chair was suddenly reclined.

Jay: Oh, yes.

Frank: So the one today was that I was going from the tilt table to the physical therapy mat, which is a raised surface; and as they were transferring me, the tilt table started separating from the mat and there was a big hole in between. A friend happened to be watching the therapy at that point. He rushed over and grabbed one end of the sheet, and the other therapist grabbed the other end, and they quickly recovered and got me on the mat!

Jay: Wow!

Frank: I don't know how close it really was, but to me it was very close and very threatening. Every time that happens it just goes right through your whole system. You realize that your whole person is being threatened; your life is being threatened, almost. If they dropped you, I don't know if it would really hurt you or not. But these mishaps happen pretty regularly, and the way to prevent them is you've got to take control. Like the time the chair went down, I let the therapist do it on the side I didn't want her to do it on. In this case, we were on this tilt table (a table which can be tilted to any angle for physical therapy) and I knew the table was not locked firmly. After it was over, the therapist said we should never do this without someone holding the table. I should have realized that beforehand. Therapists have never objected when I insisted on something like that, which is a very positive thing.

Jay: I'm impressed with the nurses. I know there've been some incidents, but basically, people really look to you for guidance.

Frank: That's not always true of my primary nurse. Sometimes she will come in and take over and turn me over or lift me up.

Jay: This is the daytime nurse?

Frank: Yeah, the primary nurse, kind of the head of the team.

Jay: She has to be in charge.

Frank: Yeah, today I came to lunch and she told me it was the Occupational Therapists who were supposed to feed me today. She kind of turned her back to me and said "That's not our job". So, meanwhile, it looked like I wasn't going to have lunch! Then somehow a student nurse came around and eventually the student fed me. But, the primary nurse is a woman who we really need to contend with, one way or another.

One time Aura was talking Spanish to the maid who is Salvadoran, and her English is not very good. So they were talking away in Spanish about different things and the maid was working and Aura was working and this nurse came in and heard the Spanish. And literally, almost shouted at the maid that we were in the United States and that we spoke English—

Jay: Ooh!

Frank: —at which point Aura fired back very quickly that we were in the United States and she was talking Spanish. She said there are millions of Americans who speak Spanish and French and different Southeast Asian languages. The nurse backed off a little, but then maintained that even her own son didn't speak any Tagalog, he spoke English. It's a continuing battle. Up to now we have been putting up with it, we are very cordial to her, take advantage of her good moods and suffer through her bad moods. But she certainly is one of the weak spots in the whole treatment program.

Jay: Is she the floor nurse or is she assigned?

Frank: She is in charge of me and she is in charge of who gets assigned to me. She can assign her best or her worst nurses or she can assign no one to me.

Jay: When I stayed overnight, a nurse came in who was the head nurse for this floor. Is your nurse over the head nurse?

Frank: Oh no. No, the head nurse of the floor, the one that was very upset that you stayed overnight, she oversees my primary nurse.

Jay: So a possibility would be to speak to her and say, look—

Frank: Yeah, well we have. But my primary nurse has been here, I think fifteen maybe twenty years, she is established. She is supposed to be a very good nurse. From their perspective, she just sometimes, you know, has bad moods. But from my perspective, it is much more serious than that. For example, obviously, one of the big issues for me is being transferred. Several times she has made remarks that nurses can hurt their backs when they transfer you.

Jay: I told that to Pierre [a mutual friend who is a MD]; he was just astounded.

Frank: Today there was a student nurse assigned to me. After the transfer was made, she went out of her way to ask the student, "Is your back okay?" This is a constant theme reminding me that people can hurt their backs when they lift me. I don't know how far we are going to go with her, or whether we are going to be able to wait it out. She seems to be itching for a fight so she can show she is in control, and this isn't a very pleasant situation in a place like this.

Jay: And you just wonder what happens to someone who meekly comes in, who can't speak, or whatever. There's a chance for catastrophe, a chance to be completely brow-beaten by the system.

Frank: No question about it. This hospital has a lot of good people in it, a lot of caring people, doctors, nurses, etc. But if you have a certain level of disability, like I have, this place can be very punishing. I can't really gauge it, or know if 'level of disability' is a thing you can quantify. But people who are in pain or can't move without assistance, or who get thirsty at night and want a drink of water or juice can wait a long time here for those services. It may be that because of my relatively good moods and humor I get more service than others.

Jay: I think that's the case. I remember when my mother was in the hospital, she talked about a night nurse who was very rude to her. In most hospitals there aren't people around. Considering the amount of latitude they give visitors here, you can imagine what it is like in most hospitals, where the visitors disappear at eight. From then on you are at the mercy of people, sensitive or insensitive—

Frank: —or even sensitive people who have a lot of needy patients. I'm always under the somewhat paradoxical view that I am so helpless, I can't do this, I can't do that, I can't move, I can't adjust my position, I can't pick something up off the floor, yet at the same time, I see people who are much, much more—I don't know if the word is unfortunate, or impacted than I. I see them all around me. I don't know what their prognosis is. I don't know how long most of them have been here.

You go for what you can get and you push for what you can get and you try to make yourself as comfortable as possible. You get the services you get, but then, on the other hand, you know that there are other patients who are needy, a lot of very elderly—80's and 90's—and some other people who are very sick. I'm not really sick. I'm in a lot of discomfort, but I'm not really sick.

Jay: I don't know what interventions you could make. You can take the director on a tour and show him the facts about not being able to use the elevator and things like that; those are changes that could be made. But there is another whole set of political changes, care changes, that aren't likely to be made in a big hospital like this.

Frank: I've never seen anyone in authority other than the director of nursing of this floor. I haven't seen the director of nursing for the building, the director of OT. And I've seen the supervisors of my two therapists, but I haven't seen or met some of the other people in charge. I don't know if I should or I shouldn't;

but I've been here a month, and I know I have been a somewhat illustrious patient.

Jay: That's a reasonable description!

Frank: There is a great separation; it is not surprising that they don't know me or see me until I do something that attracts attention. Today a woman walked by and someone said something about being the boss. I assume that she was the head of nursing for the hospital. She didn't say hello, and she didn't introduce herself, either.

Jay: I imagine that the people in the hierarchy here are under tremendous pressure.

Is that too much air coming in? Do you want me to --

Frank: I think I'm going to go to sleep, I've pretty much had it.

What's His Name? - Aura

What's his name, she asks me,
Does he have his clinic card?
I stiffen, sensing your contours fading
to the sepia of an antique photo.
Last week, the waitress at The Landing
asked me for your order.

two years ago, your body
was as strong as the pumpkin
pine driftwood on our shore
that you made
into our dining table,
as energetic as the power tools
you deftly used to make our
picture frames.

Independent, you survived
The Maine woods
with only Calamus,
your dog, for company;
you've become a third world country,
stripped of resources,
dependent on the first world

for the very crops you used to grow
abundantly.

Your professorial robes once
swiftly swishing
down the aisles of Pomp and Circumstance
are now pinned silent
like the prim bun of a cloistered nun.
Ironic
that the fast paced
squash you loved to play
would stun you into stillness.

Nerves once a part of a well-planned
scheme,
taunt you falsely,
careen like bumper cars,
inflict random pain,
thoughtlessly inviting
arctic and equatorial demons
to possess you
Yet the white-water swiftness
of your mind,
becoming your protector,
escapes this senseless sentence.

"My name is Frank," you bellow
and roll your chair away

FRANK AND JAY, TUESDAY OCTOBER 13, 1992: WALK OF THE CENTIPEDE

"You get the feeling that you're operating a puppet and the puppet is you."

Underlying Frank's tormented battles with the nursing staff and the hospital regimen was his belief that he would walk again. He resisted rules, not because he was unwilling to do the work, but because he thought they were inane, mechanical, irrelevant to his unique needs. His diligence and perseverance in the physical therapy sessions was, however, a whole other thing. Here he would work until exhaustion. Here, on the mats, he would have spent the entire day if physically able. Frank, after all, had always been a fighter and a worker. Before his injury, when he felt sick, his remedy was to go out and chop wood or play a game of squash or tennis. Yet even Frank's great enthusiasm for his physical therapy did not separate him from his ubiquitous role as observer and interpreter of this experience.

Frank: A number of weeks ago, I started sitting up at the edge of one of these mats that PT's use. That whole process of beginning to sit up, and not knowing where my mid-point or my balance point was, was very tedious, very threatening. One side of me wanted to lay down and quit and the other side said, 'Somehow I've got to do this'—and yet not quite knowing why, although now it seems so obvious. One of the most difficult, tedious things was the tilt board. But I went from total lack of confidence to now total confidence when I sit up. It's like being one of those dolls that has a round bottom with a weight in it, and when you knock it over, it always comes out right. Well, that's the way my bottom feels, I'm not really secure, but I can always right myself.

Jay: So it sounds like some of the muscles are there for balancing, but not—

Frank: —not all of them, but usually what they call the gluteus maximus, the muscles in your rear that are critical to standing and sitting and to getting up. Those are in tough shape still but they are coming in. I first stood up—just in a pivot—in a transfer; I stood up for a second and then moved over and got onto a bed. Then I stood up, with the therapist having her arms around me and guiding me, for ten, fifteen seconds. Then I proceeded to stand up over one of those mats that are built up, leaning over it. My knees would buckle and I couldn't see my knees, so it was very perilous.

Jay: On the parallel bars, what did you do at first, three days ago?

Frank: Well, they had a mirror so I could see. I stood up with a walker, to hold my arms. I stood up and battled with buckling knees; just like when I started sitting, I had no sense of balance, of orientation, of mid-point. I still don't have it. I've been standing up for three days; but I didn't have it after I had been sitting for the first three days, either, so I somehow know that's going to happen. When that happens, everything will be different.

I have to have some realization of what goes on when I'm standing up straight. I don't have a sense of posture. Sometimes when the therapist says, 'Oh, you're leaning forward', I don't even know it.

Jay: You're not experiencing feedback so you can make the self corrections. You have to make them on the basis of observations from other people.

Frank: There are several things that I'm not experiencing: the physical feedback, because I don't know what the right position is; I can't feel my feet, therefore I have to look at them in some way, and I'm not used to that kind of feedback. Visual feedback from walking and standing is something I've never had in my life, but it is the only thing I've got now.

Jay: So it makes it a more intellectual, cognitive type of experience.

Frank: You get the feeling that you're operating a puppet and the puppet is you. You have to pull the strings and straighten out the legs, pull in the chest, and they're all operating separately, they're not operating as a system. My leg is one system and my hips are another, my stomach another and my back's another system.

Jay: It's like that story you used to tell about the centipede. (A centipede was asked how it managed to coordinate its hundred legs in order to walk. It replied, "Well, first you move your first leg forward and then, ah…" Pausing to think about how it happens, it never walked again.)

Frank: Right. Absolutely. It's like I can never stand up, because at the same time I have to pull my butt in, stick my chest out, stand up straight, get my shoulders up and do something to my legs, and I have to do all those at the same time. It seems almost impossible. When I do it, they say, 'Great! You're doing a great job!' (laughter)

At one point, the therapists all clapped. Actually, that was when I first really stood up and they just clapped. Now there is no question I have the power to stand up and stay there for ten seconds, then twenty. I can do it for five minutes. But, after five minutes, I get pretty tired and my legs give way.

Jay: Your tiredness suggests how many muscles are working to keep you balanced that haven't worked in the last month.

Frank: And also how nervous I am about it. It was the same with sitting up. It's difficult, it's unsettling, it's dangerous, and all those things add up to fatigue. I guess I have gone over the edge in the sense that I really think that I'm going to walk.

Jay: Well, you did.

Frank: I did take a step or so, it was within a very close context. At the same time, supposedly, feeling is going to come back in my legs. Then it is much more likely that it will be a system rather than three or four systems.

Jay: You'd say that you are having the sense of feeling coming in slowly?

Frank: Very slowly, and not nearly as fast as the movement. I mean the muscles are coming in but the feeling is lagging behind.

Jay: The feeling is on the surface, so it sounds –

Frank: No, it's the feeling you have of your legs. What do you lose when your foot goes to sleep? You don't lose just the surface, you lose the whole sense of your leg. It's like it's not there; and my legs are, like, permanently asleep.

I'm getting some feeling on the outside which you don't get with a sleeping leg; I'm continually feeling pins and needles in my legs. Pins and needles have always preceded movement. When my toes started to move, way back, it was preceded and accompanied by pins and needles; I don't know how to explain it, something like rays or beams—very subtle feelings, and I can feel those in my legs.

Jay: Are you feeling some of that in your left arm too?

Frank: Yeah, my left arm is so far behind, I don't know whether it is going to get better or not. I really hurt it last night when they were trying to turn me and the nurse pulled the sheet up on it. I hadn't pulled it away.

Jay: Was it pinned under you or wrenched?

Frank: It was just kind of pinned under me, I guess. She pulled the sheet up to turn me over and the arm was inside that sheet.

Jay: Wow! Made more difficult by the fact that you can't always be aware of exactly where it is, since it isn't giving you a full message.

Frank: I *don't* know where it is! As a matter of fact you ought to just check on it right now. (laughs) See where it is and pick it up and just kind of readjust it a little bit.

Jay: Okay, your hand is up and it is slightly flexed, should I move it or massage it?

Frank: Just flatten the fingers out.

Jay: When I flatten your fingers out, it takes a minute for them to relax. Do you want me to put the splint on?

Frank: No, not now.

Jay: How is that now?

Frank: If you flatten the fingers they will tend to stay flat and that's a better position for them.

Jay: Your thumb is straight. There, how is that?

Frank: Okay.

Jay: That was a very vivid description of the different systems that don't connect with each other at this point.

Frank: A lot of analogies to personality and to social groups and to teaching, to therapy.

Jay: Cohesiveness.

Frank: It's kind of a metaphor of my whole experience, and I constantly get these images of families that don't work, communities that don't work, where the different pieces are working separately.

There is a very elderly agitated woman in the room next door and she keeps on yelling that she is thirsty, she is wet. I know the nurses are going in and giving her something to drink and she will immediately forget that she wanted something to drink. So she is a very difficult patient. The nurses would come in and talk to her and I became more and more aware of how they talked to her—some as a human being and some as if she were a baby.

There was one nurse, Carol, who was taking care of me. I had listened to her talk to this woman. She came in, it must have been three or four in the morning. I said, "Carol, you should listen to yourself talking to a patient, particularly that patient." She said, "Oh?" I said, "I don't know if you're aware of it but you really treat her like a human being, and a lot of the nurses, even the good nurses, don't." She was interested in what I meant by that. I said, "Well, you're interested in what, even in her agitated state, she thinks, and you give her credit for being a person. You should be in my position here and listen to the ways some other people talk to her, like she was an infant or an inanimate object."

I'm trying to talk the head nurse into doing a little study on how nurses talk to patients and she was kind of interested in it. The only question is, how do you get those tapes. Whether you get everyone's permission, I don't know, but the raw material is there. I've seen that in teachers talking to kids. You see it all the time—professors talking to students—but in hospitals it's exacerbated. It is totally polarized, because some of the patients are so out of it. This agitated and, you might say, somewhat deranged woman often does not make sense, but you know, it is just as true as when they talk to me, when they talk to some articulate person: some people come in and say " Okay, Deary" and proceed right along. I am an object and I'm treated like an object.

Jay: It strikes me that the person who comes in and calls you 'Deary' is trying to avoid the pain, the energy loss, of really being with people.

At this point two nurses enter the room. Frank has been lying face down on his bed with his arms at his side for the last half hour and it is time to turn him over on his back before he goes to sleep. Turning him over is a difficult maneuver, both for the nurses and for Frank, who has learned to direct those who turn him so that his arms are not injured in the process. They stand, one on each side of the bed while Jay stands close

by, ready to assist as needed. One of these nurses is Natasha, who often takes care of Frank.

Nurse: What do you think, Frank?

Frank: I'm ready to go.

Nurse: All right.

Frank: What I have to do is be brought over to the left hand side of the bed, and then this arm goes up, and then—it's very easy to turn me back, if you just don't touch that arm.

Nurse: Okay, you want to get pushed over towards the window or towards us?

Frank: Towards us.

Natasha: (taking charge of the procedure): First take the pillow and—

Frank: (to first nurse, who is starting the turn-over incorrectly.) No, no, no!

Natasha: You pull him with this (gesturing to the sheet underneath Frank).

Frank: If you do that, my face goes right—

Natasha: Okay. One, two—all the way here. (pulling the sheet towards herself)

Frank: Watch my arm, watch my arm!

Natasha: I've got your arm, it's over here.

Frank: Okay.

Nurse: All right. What should I do with it?

Frank: Wait a second. There isn't enough room on my right, yet. We need more....Okay, a little bit more. Is there any more room? (between his body and the edge of the bed)

Nurses: No.

Natasha: Your legs are hanging off the bed.

Frank: From my body, you can begin turning me.

Nurse: What should I do with your arm, Frank?

Frank: Oh, I'll take care of that.

Natasha: Ok, one, two— (the nurses turn him over onto his back)

Frank: Okay, that did it.

Natasha: Okay, now I'm going to pull the sheet. (to center Frank on the bed)

Frank: Natasha, get my arm. No, my left arm, my left arm, very gently. Now, just put it down, great.

Natasha: Now we could fix the sheets down?

Frank: Yeah, that was great.

The two nurses brush Frank's teeth, give him his medications for the night and discuss plans for waking him in the night to use the urinal and for catheterizing him in the morning.

Nurse: Good night, thanks, Jay, for your help.

Jay: You're welcome. (The nurses leave) I realize, as we do this, how much detail there is to each thing. You could have a manual that thick on what has to happen. And it would probably get revised each day, too. Shall I put a sheet over you, are you ready?

Frank: Yeah, but don't cover up my feet.

Jay: To remember all that is a lot!

Being With Frank: Part 1

Visitors flooded Frank's room when I first came to see him at the rehabilitation hospital; despite his predicament, he seemed to enjoy entertaining the crowd. I recalled the parties he and Aura threw at their home in Winthrop, wall to wall with people. I had hoped to find out how he was coping with his injury, but the gathering precluded our communication. I left, wanting to visit at a time when we could talk. Later, Frank would tell me that he didn't want to drive his friends away by revealing the depths to which his loss of independence could take him.

I believed that, faced with his paralysis and the prospect of long-term hospitalization, Frank would want to reflect about his altered existence. Since we had shared a lot in the past, I felt he would be open with me. Many times during the years we worked together—after a class, a faculty meeting, a game of tennis or squash, or when in his or my office at the end of the day—we had discussed broader issues than those of work. Frank had a way of opening up a topic to its controversies, ironies and fundamental properties. While he took strong positions, his passion was always moderated by a sense of fairness. He respected the nuances in a situation lending an investigative tone to our conversations. I had enjoyed discovering the reflective Frank and appreciated his willingness to explore any topic.

Over the years that we worked together, a chemistry between us generated an atmosphere of mischief and adventure. Once, when visiting several bilingual classrooms in a public school in Miami, we noticed that they were segregated from the rest of the building. The curriculum seemed unimaginative, more focused on controlling pupils than on offering opportunities for exploratory learning. Afterward we met with a principal eager to hear about what we had observed. I had noted that the shades in these classrooms had been drawn so that the children couldn't look out the window. Risking his displeasure, I told the principal that drawing the shades in the classroom reminded me of putting a cloth over a cage in order to keep birds quiet. The principal beamed. "Yes, yes!" he said. "It is very similar to what we are trying to do with these children". I looked at Frank out of the corner of my eye and saw, to my delight, that he was trying to suppress a smile. Afterwards, walking down the street outside the building, we broke into gales of laughter.

After several visits to the hospital, I realized that I could help out by joining Frank at night, when other visitors were absent and nurses were less available. Aura, worried about his being alone, started spending the night with him, sleeping on a mattress on the floor beside his bed. As she also spent much of the day at the hospital, she needed relief, and I offered to take her place beside Frank on occasional evenings or nights.

I was in awe of the enormity Frank faced. How could I accompany one whose life now differed so profoundly from mine? I arose in the morning without thinking about each movement of my body or how to withstand flashes of pain, without dependence on the assistance of others. I did not find myself in situations where protection from further serious injury might lie in the hands of a stranger. These differences appeared to create a gulf between me and Frank; I placed him on a pedestal of tragedy. Who was I to think that I had anything to offer him? Inclined to see people as managing their own situation and therefore not needing my help, I'm apt to hold back, reluctant to enter unbidden into another's private domain.

My hesitation soon dissolved. On my second visit to the hospital, I ran into Aura in the lobby as she was leaving. She hugged me, with tears streaming down her face, and I realized how completely Frank's injury had overwhelmed her. She desperately needed support for Frank and for herself. I needn't worry so much about intruding.

I also thought about the challenges Frank faced. His injury had cast him adrift from everything familiar. Like a refugee fleeing his country, Frank needed to orient himself to a new life. He learned some things from meetings with physicians and therapists, but their prognosis was uncertain. He could gain information from fellow patients, especially those with similar injuries. However, I believed in Frank's innate capacity to assess things. Conversation might serve as a means by which Frank might best evaluate his condition and his new environment, a hunch confirmed by his request that he and I find time to talk about his experiences in the hospital.

As a therapist, I like listening to my clients as they tell their stories. Removed from memory's vault, the story assumes a life of its own and opens itself to the speaker. Telling deepens and enriches a story as memories and insights emerge. Along the way, I may question or comment about those aspects of the story which have drawn me in. When I do my work well, the story itself guides the therapy. I imagined that—with this approach—Frank could talk freely about all that had happened since he had crashed into the wall of the squash court ten days earlier.

It felt as if I were going on a camping trip without equipment or map when I arrived for my first overnight stay with Frank. Would I know how to help him prepare for sleep? How much of this would be performed by nurses? Where would I sleep; how often should I check on Frank? Would I be able to sleep, in the stifling heat and noise of the hospital? Maybe I had bitten off more than I could chew. I also felt a certain fierce delight in taking on the challenge. And I knew that, somehow, despite his pain and paralysis, Frank would include me as a partner on this adventure.

Participating in the process of preparing Frank for bed catapulted me into both witnessing and performing the most basic functions, from moving his arms and legs or brushing his teeth to checking to see whether the catheter was firmly attached to his penis. To my relief, Frank knew what would enable him to get what little sleep he could. The aide assisting that evening and I often failed to follow his instructions in positioning him for sleep, as I was new and so, it seemed, was she. Frequently one of us would touch him or move his body in a way that hurt. Frank's exclamations quickly informed us of our blunders, leaving me uncertain about my skills as a night nurse.

After Frank was settled, the head nurse banished me to the waiting area a few doors down the corridor. I slept on a mattress on the floor, my head close to the open door so that I could hear Frank, a few doors away, and check on him, between periods of dozing. The night was a tussle between a desire for sleep and worry about whether I would hear Frank's calls to have a blanket added or removed, a pillow adjusted, a glass of water provided or a nurse summoned. In the morning, Frank, stiff from lying in bed all night, asked me to stretch his legs. When Aura arrived I sped home, eager for sleep and relieved that Frank and I had survived the night together.

Having managed that initial venture, I assumed a rhythm of weekly overnight stays with Frank, scheduling my clients the next day to allow for some sleep. Thus began a series of late-evening conversations in which Frank and I reflected on his experiences as a quadriplegic patient at the hospital. We met in Frank's hospital room that, for the most part, he shared with roommates. Usually there would be an opportunity to chat with Frank's evening visitors before they left. Occasionally we moved to the solarium, which looked out over the Charles River, bordered with ribbons of white and red lights as late commuters made their way home. After we returned to Frank's room I would turn the tape recorder on and he would begin by reviewing the events since the last time we had met.

Evenings afforded us a natural opportunity to talk as the hospital corridors quieted after the day's activity. The boisterous Frank who entertained his visitors emerged naturally, but so did the reflective Frank who faced an altered life. The ritual of taking medications (usually at about 10 PM), being arranged in his bed, having a snack or a drink and the other preparations for sleep reminded me of how bedtime stories and talking had allowed my sons Peter and David to wind down from the events of the day. At times I gave Frank a hug (carefully, because of his new sensitivity to being touched) after we had finished talking.

Except for the moments of disorientation when, heavily medicated, he became confused about what country he was in, Frank's mind remained as active as ever, in contrast to his physical limitations. Reflection allowed him to roam, free of the need for support or direction. Yet expression of the mind requires a medium. As Frank declared in our first conversation, he possessed neither the hands to write with nor the will to dictate. He needed a friend with whom he could talk.

Frank, through the force of his personality and seniority— nearly ten years older than I—usually provided the framework for our conversations. Never before had I visited someone whose life had been shattered by severe injury. Never had I been involved, except with family members, in caring for the physical needs of another over an extended period of time. In a subtle reversal— Frank having been my mentor— I felt that I now fulfilled a nurturing role: that of listening to Frank and facilitating the exploration of whatever topics he raised.

Frank wanted to get to the bottom of things. He wished to understand the specific nature of his injury. He sought to learn about the workings of the hospital. And he reflected on how he had dealt with both physical and political obstacles as he reviewed with me the events of the day.

I had always been surprised at the intensity of Frank's preoccupations. His wide-ranging interests had included reading fiction and the adventure of travel. He loved to work around the house, building furniture or making repairs, drawing on his enormous armory of tools. He enjoyed quiet moments in wilderness as much he did raucous parties. Now his focus drew in upon his body and the hospital environment as he struggled to survive his ordeal. Perhaps in private moments Frank's thoughts still roamed far a-field, but in my presence, he seemed to have relinquished many outside interests. Who among us, faced with similar circumstances would not retreat to survival's essentials?

Later, I was amazed at Frank's ability to explore the larger implications of patient versus hospital, but at the beginning, he turned his attention to the micro world of steps—tiny for me, immense for him—leading toward improvement. In jokingly asking the visiting Dean of the School of Education whether his newly acquired ability to wiggle his toes was worth a publication, Frank captured the difference between the dimensions of his old and new worlds.

The hospital setting provided a changing yet consistent context for our conversation. Hospital staff regularly entered Frank's room, especially in the evenings when he was preparing for sleep. On a few occasions his roommate drifted into our conversation when he awoke from a nap. Often Frank would interrupt to ask for assistance with some physical need, and I became more attentive to situations requiring my help, such as when the pad which prevented his elbow from chafing slipped down his arm. Our talks began to move easily back and forth between intellectual, political, emotional and physical concerns. These evening routines of nurses' visits, medications and preparations for sleep offered a rhythmic background for a conversation about Frank's rehabilitation that continued for three months.

I considered it an honor that Frank opened himself up to me as he spoke of his wonder at all that was happening to him. Everything we discussed seemed essential. I assume that for him our conversations provided the perspective necessary to plunge back into the rigors of hospitalization. Our conversations brought us to moments of deep pain as well as triumph, when only tears, silence or occasionally laughter would suffice as Frank spoke of his "roller coaster" ride. Sometimes I shared my own experiences of loss and pain; at other times I struggled to be with him when the agonies of which he spoke were beyond my comprehension. For me, our dialogue afforded a rare form of friendship and a reminder that much of what I take for granted is extraordinary and precious and could be removed forever in an instant.

FRANK AND JAY, THURSDAY, OCTOBER 15, 1992: "POWERFUL MEANS CHANGING THE WAY YOU LOOK AT THINGS"

Frank: One thing that I have been thinking about is what you might call the McMurphy syndrome, from *One Flew Over the Cuckoo's Nest*. I look at the patients around here; a lot of them are depressed, looking at the ceiling and not taking an active part in anything. I have begun talking to one Chinese kid, an engineer, who is totally depressed and whenever you ask him, "How's it going?" he never says it is going very well. I've always been curious about when you go someplace and someone asks, "How's it going?" You can almost control something by saying, "Ah, terrible!" or you can say "It's going great!"—disregarding how you feel.

There's another guy down at the end of the hall, Mike, and sometimes he can say it wasn't too bad of a day, but that's the best he can do. Maybe they're not experiencing any elation in what is happening to them and maybe they got no place to go, but I think it's more their attitude, their posture, and I think the hospital encourages it. Much like in *The Cuckoo's Nest*: they all met in that group, if you remember. I'm interested in re-reading the book or re-seeing the film, because I get all of these images and, in fact, I see some of the same people here.

As I remember, the reaction to McMurphy was to try and calm him down, to silence and eventually extinguish him. This primary nurse of mine is always doing that to me. I want to get up all the time, so she puts down transfers, saying how much her back hurts or someone else's back hurts when they do it; so that, somehow, I don't think it is conscious—I'll feel guilty or I won't ask for transfers as often. A few days ago, I went to bed at 2:30 PM and she said, "OK you're down for the night." (laughs). I was just going down to get catheted and do some exercises and then I was going to get back up again. An awful lot of the people here get up in a chair for an hour or two a day, or get up for therapy and then they are back down again.

Jay: If they're down, then they're inactive, passive and regimented. The corridor and rooms like this often don't have any place where the people can gather and talk with one another. Visitors come and talk, but dialogue is not part of the agenda.

Frank: Absolutely. Half the time, the curtains are pulled and there is a nurse in there. Today I wheeled into the Chinese engineer's room, and he was kind of surprised, but smiling, and we talked a little. It struck me that here's this hospital, with nurses and doctors, physical therapists and occupational therapists, social workers who do intake and outtake—and, as far as I know—there isn't a single rehab counselor in the hospital. There is no one here counseling people about how their past and their present connect with their future. No one is exploring what they could become excited about and look forward to doing. So that when someone asks, "How do you feel?", they'd really say, "Yeah, I feel fine; my ass hurts and my stomach hurts, and my leg hurts, but I did this".

What they do have here, which is reminiscent of *The Cuckoo's Nest*, are social groups. Usually there is a note on the board. This guy comes in who is a volunteer, and asks me if I'm going to go to the social group at 5:15, we are going to make paper airplanes or stuff like that. Well, the therapy group in *The Cuckoo's Nest* is a little different, a little more directed. But mainly it's passivity. (Frank begins to cough and sniffle).

Jay: Are you all right? I could blow your nose! (laughs)

Frank: Wait a minute! We didn't write that into the contract! We said you could come as many times as you want, but you can't blow my fucking nose! (laughter)

This whole business [the hospital's policy of getting patients to bed by 9:30-10 PM], has clearly taken precedence over my desire to be active, make tapes and talk to people. It's right up that theme of an institution that either tries to get people out, or tries to get people to fit into a certain way of life, a certain culture, a certain posture.

The last few days, I have been walking, with braces and with a lot of assistance from nurses, but walking down the hall. One person, the patients' rep, told me that she walked by and saw it and was very excited, but she didn't want to show it. She walked into her office and told her assistant, "Mr. Garfunkel is walking! I can't get over it!" But she walked right by me and didn't show it.

On the other hand, this psychiatrist I know—and he knows me quite well, I knew him ten years ago—I noticed him walk by me two or three times and never look at me, never show any recognition of it. It was like that *New Yorker* cartoon where everyone is smiling except one face is grim, or the other way around. I just try to figure out how this fits in, because the therapists are all excited about my walking. But you don't see any excitement in anyone else. As far as I am concerned it's not because patients can't do things, and are not making progress. It's this 'no celebration' policy.

Jay: Maybe you are the property of the PT when you are walking. When you're sitting on the pot, you are the property of someone else. There isn't really a team.

Frank: There is no team. There is no time. It's not part of the culture. Today, the patients' representative said, "Oh, we are going to have a team meeting." I said, "You are out of touch with the place! It's your place but--."

There is a way around it, and that is mini teams. If you identify a problem with my hands, for example, and that is the problem of the OT, maybe the OT and the doctor can meet with me and talk about what they're doing. That's not really a team, but at least I'm involved in the decision. It's very difficult for them to involve me in decisions. It's not part of the culture; it's not the way they do things. I'm overcoming it because I'm a professional and have the verbal skills and everything. If the Chinese kid were involved in the discussion of what they're doing with him and how they're doing it, maybe he could get excited about what he *could* do, rather than getting depressed about what he *can't* do.

Jay: Anyone who is a patient here is having a very powerful experience. The more you don't talk about it, the more it gets lodged inside you and begins to eat away at you. It almost seems as if dialogue is the most important part of the therapy.

Frank: I'm not so sure I agree with you that everyone in this place is having a powerful experience. For some people that's the trouble; it's not a powerful experience. It's depressing, it's—

Jay: —but that's a powerful experience.

Frank: Powerful for me means *changing* the way you look at things, *changing* the way you react, *changing* the meanings of things.

Jay: Yes, and that's all happening, even if you're sitting in a room by yourself and no one's paying any attention to you. Your meaning system is going to change. You're getting to the point where you feel powerless, that no one cares about you, that nothing's going to change. Even if you say something or make a move, it's not going to make any difference.

Frank: I think they're just continuing their lives, though, a lot of them. You see, I feel profoundly affected. I think you would agree that I'm talking about things in ways that I touched on before in my life, but they never went through the core of me. This one guy, Mike, told me that he weighed three hundred and sixty pounds, he was diabetic, he had high cholesterol, that he smoked three packs of cigarettes a day; he's a walking time bomb. He doesn't particularly like to get up; he was complaining about his therapy. When you ask him how things are going, there seems to be very little there. I think there was very little before. The experience of being in the hospital hasn't gotten to him. If it got to him one of two things would happen: He'd be out of his fucking mind or he'd be looking at things in a different light.

Hi, dear!

(Nurse comes in, tape turned off)

* * *

Frank: One night they started to turn me over and I thought there was something wrong. Now I know that it's just impossible to get turned over in the middle of the night. They don't have any staff to watch you, they have people who've never done it before. But I let them start, and in the middle of it there was a discussion when I said, "Well, move me over to my left". Someone said "Well, which is the left?" (laughter) And I said, "*Wait* a minute! (laughter) Wait a minute!" So I stopped it; I said "Why don't you forget about it." And they said, "We have an order to do it." I said, "Well, now you have an order not to do it!" Did we discuss the time they turned me over and hurt me?

Jay: Yes, that sounded pretty grim, because I was here the next night and she was here and she was able to laugh about it.

Frank: Well, she is just a marvelous person. She's not here tonight but ordinarily she's the one that transfers me; she's the one that turns me over. She just sits around and talks and jokes and is lovely, as quite a few of them are, but she's in a special place.

One of the things that occurs to me is I've developed these relationships. Maybe when I leave here I'll never see or hear from these people again; but with a bunch of women, all the way from young women to those in their thirties and forties, they're touching relationships, they're hugging relationships. You know, the only woman I hug is Aura —well, there are a few other people, like a doctoral student who has done a dissertation, who I might hug. But suddenly these people have entered into my life in very personal, warm, supportive ways; they see my penis, they see me in great pain but also in great laughter, there's a whole bunch of them.

You go along from month to month and year to year and occasionally you meet new people. Occasionally some person or couple comes along that you get close to. Usually it's a small bunch of people you have special relationships with. But here's another bunch that I have very special relationships with—even more so, now that I'm kind of pushing them. Today the physical therapist kept saying, "Are you tired, are you tired?" There's *no* way I could be tired, no way in the world I could be tired; in a way, no way in the world someone could ask that question. I mean they had to ask it, but—actually she said, "Well, I'm tired, why don't you sit down for awhile." I don't think that they could have gotten me tired had they walked me for a full hour.

BEING WITH FRANK: PART 2

I met Frank in the spring of 1967, when I applied for a faculty position in the Department of Special Education at Boston University. At that time Frank directed a graduate program preparing masters and doctoral students to work with emotionally disturbed children. Having participated in team teaching during my graduate years, I sought a setting in which I could collaborate closely with colleagues. I remember liking Frank's plan for my interview, including meetings with groups of students and faculty, and joint observations of two laboratory classrooms that operated within the department. Clearly, he wanted to learn what I saw when I observed a classroom and how I interacted with others. His approach seemed to be: 'let's throw Jay in with these people and classrooms and see how he engages with them'. While Frank put a lot of thought into designing classes and programs, he cherished space in which things could happen spontaneously. He perceived randomness and serendipity as effective disclosers of people and institutions.

I saw Frank as someone whose openness and enthusiasm would support my initiatives, who would collaborate rather than direct, and whose curiosity was vigorous. In the fourteen years of teaching at BU that followed, my initial impressions were surpassed. I admired Frank's originality and his readiness to challenge those in positions of power. He supported my establishing a series of programs (funded by the US Office of Education to prepare junior high school teachers to work with special needs pupils being integrated into their classrooms) and challenged me to expand my thinking and writing. I delighted in his cynical, irreverent sense of humor, ready to challenge the pompous or the proper.

During the fall of my first year at BU, we played tennis several times. On one occasion my ball landed in his court, close to the line, but clearly *in* as I saw it. He called it *out*. I challenged his call. Frank bristled at my presumption. "You bug the shit out of me", he roared. "You bug the shit out of me", I yelled back. From that moment forward our friendship was cemented. Despite our age difference, we contended with each other as equals.

Frank savored unexpected moments of beauty or adventure. Once, we traveled to Gainesville, Florida to attend a conference for directors of graduate programs in Special Education. On the last day of the conference, Frank proposed that we skip the rest of the proceedings, hop in our rented car and visit the Okeefenokee Swamp before catching our flight back to Boston. We rented a small motorboat and headed out on a creek into the midst of the wilderness. Soon trees surrounded us, some covered with Spanish moss, others with their brilliant orange leaves reflected in the still water. We turned the engine off and for several hours became absorbed in a world of color and silence. Suddenly I looked at my watch. We would make it to the airport in time to catch our flight if we left immediately. But the boat's outboard engine wouldn't start. Each of us took turns trying to coax the cranky motor, Frank laughing uproariously, while I laughed at his laughter, relinquishing my anxiety over our delay. For Frank it was a moment of existential splendor, surrounded by the wildness and beauty of the swamp and the total uncertainty of our circumstances.

I came to appreciate that in addition to Frank's bravado existed a sensitivity to moments of crisis and an ability to act with compassion. On one occasion a doctoral student had scheduled a hearing on her dissertation proposal. Shortly before the date, a faculty member resigned from her committee and was replaced by another whom she did not know well. At the hearing the new member raised questions about her research design. Already unsettled by the last-minute change, the student burst into tears. The hearing became a shambles. Frank, attending as an observer, quietly took charge, pointing out the strengths of the proposal and offering a framework for addressing the questions being raised. Bolstered by Frank's intervention, the student was able to regain her composure and complete her hearing.

When our eldest son, Peter, was born with a serious heart defect requiring immediate surgery, Frank, attending professional conferences on the West Coast, kept in daily contact with colleagues in order to learn about his progress. Seven years later, when Peter died suddenly of related complications, Frank established a fund to support the distribution of a book about hospitalization that Kitty had written for two-and-a-half-year-old Peter, before he underwent a second heart surgery at the Mayo Clinic.

Fundamental to Frank's character was a desire to get to the truth. He challenged the conventional when he suspected a disregard of evidence and a lack of critical thought. He sought the collision of ideas because he believed that the tension between opposing points of view brought essential questions into sharper focus. For Frank, irony, sarcasm and, at times, insult, served as a summons to the lists of intellectual combat. Dispute was a means to enhance understanding and litigation was an arena in which the powerful and the powerless could meet on equal footing.

Frank's presence in our department humanized my time at Boston University. His commitment to an open, supportive atmosphere of collegiality among both students and faculty fostered a sense of joint endeavor that nourished my professional growth. Frank's disgust with the games played by those seeking favor with academic authorities reduced much of the political warfare that seemed to absorb the lives of faculty members in other departments of the School of Education. Working closely with this extraordinary man brought humor, enterprise and a sense of belonging into my life. Once, after a visit by Frank to a summer camp for emotionally disturbed children where I was working as a psychologist, a friend observed "You light up like a Christmas tree whenever Frank is around!"

FRANK AND JAY, SATURDAY OCTOBER 17, 1992: "MAYBE YOU NEED THE ADVERSITY"

Frank: The last time I got on my stomach was this morning. As the nurse left, I said, "Please check up on me regularly." She said, "Okay". Then she left. After about ten or fifteen minutes, I started getting nervous that the buzzer was slipping out of my hand; my mouth was on the mattress, so I rang the bell. No one responded.

I started getting afraid, not because I was in danger, but what if I did get in danger? What if I needed help? So I put the light on. No response for 15 minutes, 20, 25 minutes. I couldn't even tell what time it was, actually. Maybe it was a minute-and-a-half.

Jay: But it felt like 25.

Frank: So then I called out for help and no one responded.

Jay: No one was in the bed here at that time?

Frank: My roommate was here, but he can't really help out in that situation. I heard some woman in the next room repeating something; no one was paying any attention to her. Some guy in the room across the hall was asking for a priest. Another guy was just talking to himself. But no nurses, no nothing. It was Kafkaesque!

I eventually yelled out, "CAN ANYONE HELP?? ANY ASSISTANTS OR NURSE AROUND?" The woman was saying she was wet, she needed a nurse. Which she says all the time, and no one pays any attention to her. Then I realized, (chuckles) there's just a *void* out there. There's nothing there, with all these people asking for help, asking for a priest, asking for anything! It went on for a long time because, finally, when the nurse, Cathy, did come in, I had been on my stomach for forty-five minutes. She said, "I'm sorry, but I went walking down the hall and a patient called me and I got tied up." Which always happens.

Jay: Are there less people around on Saturday?

Frank: Yeah, there's less people around on weekends. During the week there must be ten therapists on the floor during the day, in addition to the nursing staff. So they'll help, they'll always help. I think there are more nurses around, too.

Jay: It's like you were invisible: You thought you were yelling and no one could hear. Or else they were deaf. Very scary.

Frank: I don't know what to do about that. I don't think I should be left alone when I'm on my stomach.

Jay: What time was that?

Frank: Probably 9:30 to 10:30: Cathy finally came back and apologized, and she proceeded to turn me over, straighten me out and get me dressed, and everything. But nevertheless, those lapses are really scary. You could have one of them when you really needed help and you would not get it. The psychiatrist told me that he had a patient that yelled and yelled and the nurses finally called him. He went down there and said to the patient, "Why do you yell?" He said, "It's the only way I can get attention," and the psychiatrist said, "What do you mean, why don't you just push the button to call the nurse?" So the patient said, "Okay, you push the button." The doctor pushed the nurse's button and they sat there for a half an hour. The psychiatrist was infuriated, but of course he can do nothing about it. (voice fades off).

Jay: You're sleepy, I think. You've had a long day.

Frank: Well —

Jay: —we can do whatever you want; if you want to sleep for a while, that's fine.

Frank: (awakening after a few moments of sleep) The other story was the walking today, and that was even with my arm in such bad shape. (from being wedged underneath him while being weighed that morning) After that incident I didn't think I'd ever be able to walk today, which really upset me because walking depends on your two arms being on the walker. Nevertheless, I was going to try it, so I got on the walker and I had a different therapist.

For the last three days I had been walking, but I was not coordinated. My body did not know what the therapists wanted me to do. Whenever I tried to do what I thought I should do, I struggled and nothing would happen—my feet wouldn't move. But somehow we kept on walking for those three days and then today, somehow, my body had some insight and I suddenly started doing a bunch of things. I started walking, coordinated—

Jay: Really!

Frank: —I mean it looked awkward but it was—

Jay: —there was an inner coordination—

Frank: —I started doing the right thing and the foot started going forward and then I would lean over and the other foot would go forward and then I would lean over and the other foot would go forward (laughing). It was fucking crazy, and I suddenly started getting the beginning of a sense of balance, and they did not have to keep on telling me what to do.

Meanwhile Aura was recording the thing on video. And some guy who I met down in the lobby when I was hanging out one day downstairs, came up, and I said, "I'm going to walk, if you want to come along." So he came along and watched the whole thing and it was interesting, both with an observer and as a central figure in it (laughs).

Jay: Now, were people holding on to you while you were doing this?

Frank: I was in the hall with the walker; there was a therapist in front of me and one in back of me. The one in back of me was continually remarking, "You know I'm hardly touching you." The three days before that, there were therapists around me and struggling with me, pushing me this way and that way and trying to get me to do the right thing.

Oh, one thing did happen the day before. We were at the end of the session and the therapists were all worn out. I wanted to go on for hours. They said, "We're just going to go to the end of the hall." But instead of taking a step and resting, and taking another step, and another step, we did six steps: boom, boom, boom, boom! It was almost running. Everyone laughed and they undid the knee bolting in one brace and they got me down and then undid the knee in the other. So that was the end of that session—that quick, rapid-fire thing. And then, today, I started really walking with some kind of rhythm, a reciprocal movement.

Jay: What's interesting is that that comes after the trauma of no one hearing your call for help. And that time you sat up without any support was also after the trauma of nearly flipping out of the chair on your head.

Frank: Yeah.

Jay: So, I don't know whether that's just happenstance or whether (chuckles) …the tension of that, and then relaxing. It's interesting.

Frank: Interesting and scary! (laughs)

Jay: Yes! (laughs)

Frank and Jay discuss the fact that the tape recorder is not on voice activation, a mode which conserves tape space, as it only records when someone is speaking. This leads to the following exchange:

Jay: That may explain why there was so much space left on the tape. With voice actualization, it's really very economical

Frank: I like that! Did you hear what you said? 'Voice actualization'!

Jay: Oh, it's voice activation. (laughter) Or whatever, the hell, it is! (laughter)

Frank: 'Actualization' like in 'self actualization'. That's what I'm striving for.

(Returning to the uneven pace of his progress): At the same time, I finally got control of my bladder. My hands are terrible; my arm is terrible. (laughs) And I'm walking with rhythm! I can't make sense out of it! Jesus Christ! You'd think I'd steadily go on towards getting some stuff back. Even if it's slow. Just proceeding to do more with my legs and, eventually, more with my hands. But now my fucking arm went out and my shoulder has to go fucking crazy!

Jay: And you're getting more pins and needles in the shoulder? What is the sensation?

Frank: It's just a mess. The doctor came in yesterday and said he thought I had a pulled muscle in my shoulder. They took x-rays to find out whether there's anything broken, or out of place. There may be something wrong with the socket. Part of that is due to the fact that the muscles are weak and are not holding it in properly; therefore these little traumas or jolts from being turned in the bed or weighed pull it out, and the natural muscle tendency to pull it in isn't working.

Jay: So, are there things now that you can't do with your arm that you were doing?

Frank: Oh, yeah. I can't do anything anymore. I can lift it slightly. Finger activity has gone down to almost nil. And there is great pain—sometimes very sensitive, sometimes numb. The doctor really didn't seem so concerned about it. I was afraid it was a real set-back. He just described the fact that the muscles weren't working properly.

Jay: But it doesn't keep the nerve regeneration from going on? I suppose that's the key thing.

Frank: If the physical therapists can get the muscles in action, supposedly, they will hold the joint in place. But there may be inflammation.

The people doing the weighing didn't know anything about the bad arm. The doctor comes in and he says what he's going to do about it, like hot packs and anti inflammatory medicine. But apparently, he didn't write it into the order. This system isn't quite together, unless the patient puts it together. (laughs) Like placing that sling on my arm. Nurse comes in and she says, "I haven't done this in years!" (laughs) Well who the fuck's going to do it!

Jay: It would be ideal if you were in a Stryker Frame. Because the transfers in and out of the chair are not traumatic; it's only when you have to be rolled over.

Frank: Stryker Frame? What's that?

Jay: You're on an axis. And so you can just be rotated. The whole bed is rotated.

Frank: Like a rotisserie. (laughs)

Jay: No—well that's interesting, because then the mattress would be on top of you, actually. (laughs) They use it for patients who are turning from one side to the other.

Frank: If my arms were okay, it would be nothing. It somehow strikes me that some kind of mystical business is going on when I make all this progress and can stand up, and at the same time my arm really seems to be going under.

Jay: It seems like the more adversity there is, the more progress you make.

Frank: Maybe you need the adversity. Or maybe if I didn't have the adversity, I'd make even more progress.

Jay: That's right. (laughs). Two very different frames.

Frank: Bruce [a colleague] was here last night. I really was in terrible pain, both my backside and my shoulder. But I didn't show it. There were a number of people in the solarium, I forget who was there. It was all very pleasant, and yet I was miserable, especially in my backside. Jesus, it felt like piece of steel—hot steel—was on it, wow! So I finally told Aura, "I guess I've got to get in bed. I don't know if it'll be any better, but it can't get any worse." So I came [back to my room]. I was kind of holding it all in. And Bruce came in. Aura started dismantling the chair. I gave her some instruction. Then she made fun of it or did something sarcastic, like when you tell someone something that they already know.

Jay: Um hmm.

Frank: Like you'll do with your wife or your kids, and they'll look at you and be disgusted that maybe you didn't have faith in them or something. She combated my telling her what to do. Ordinarily that happens all the time, and it goes off our back. But I just fell apart (cries). I told her I couldn't fight her. So she kind of consoled me. Bruce witnessed that, and he suddenly saw the other side of the experience. I realized that a lot of people have never seen that, because I've hidden it from them or it just didn't come about when they were here. I was glad he didn't walk out; some people would have. He stayed and he, too, consoled me. I got back in bed. Calmed down a little bit. But I'm wondering about the fact that it is pretty tough stuff.

Jay: Yes.

Frank: People get reports that I'm walking one day (chuckles), standing up, took five steps, took ten steps. Not that I care very much, but I'm curious about the perception. I don't know if they should really know how tough it is. I guess I'm just saying that there's probably a very distorted perception, I guess there has to be.

Jay: Unless they have been through it themselves.

Frank: Right.

Jay: It's pretty hard for them to realize what a roller coaster it is. I imagine it's like being a P.O.W., that after a while it gets to you. There are times when it just gets to you. There's no other way about it. The people who only want to see you as getting better and better all the time probably will deny that. Other people, who have been through that kind of thing in some way, know that—You all right?

Frank: I'm just trying to identify where my legs are; I don't know what they're doing. I don't know whether they're lying on the bed or sticking straight up in the air.

Jay: Lying on the bed, they're under the sheets; they're tucked in a bit.

Frank: Um hmm. So I don't know whether I want people to know how miserable (chuckles) I am—I don't think that's it— if they want to talk about it, and take an interest in me, I want them to know something that's not too distorted.

Jay: Um hmm.

Frank: I'm not going to obsess about the pain. I tell Aura what's going on, but I don't tell anyone else what's going on, except a doctor or a nurse.

Jay: I imagine that the breakdowns are absolutely necessary to survive the God damn thing. It's not a matter of being as tough as steel. You can't go on like that.

Frank: It came up with Ed [a mutual friend], too. I was telling him that I was having some bad moments. He said, "Gee, you've been upbeat when I've been here." (laughs) Well, part of the reason I was upbeat was because he was there! (laughs) And that's true of a lot of people; I'm upbeat because they come.

Jay: I know, from talking with Ed, that he really feels your pain. I don't sense in him a desire to have you be a certain way. You're saying it, but—

Frank: I don't know exactly what I'm saying.

Jay: What I hear you saying is that there are times when the pain and the frustration are overwhelming. It's a question of how much of that do you let people in on.

Frank: Um hmm.

Jay: Most people know, from their own pain—not that it's been the same as yours. Recovery from anything is not a simple thing. I go back to the experience with Peter [his death]. There would be days when I'd be up and days when I'd be thrown right back, as if I were starting all over again. I can look back and see a recovery process, but that wasn't what I experienced at the time. It engulfs you.

Frank: (softly) Real pain.

Jay: Even then, my words—as I think back on it—are not the same as the experience.

Frank: And then there's other people's perception of you and your experience, most of it projections. But then, you have to go on.

Jay: You have to go on, yes. But part of what permits you to go on is having to yield to the pain and craziness of it, at times. You don't stay there, you pick up and go on. But it's after a breakdown, after a relapse or whatever. 'Relapse' isn't the word; 'breakdown' is closer.

Frank: I also get the feeling, too—I don't know that it's any less true with grieving—how slow it is. How ambiguous.

Jay: Um hmm

Frank: The fact that I'm walking looks like great progress. On the other hand, I still can't pick up a glass of water or do hardly anything for myself. I still lie in bed here and if the phone's an inch further than it should be, I can't answer it. If the nurse's button is a *fraction* further away, and I lurch for it, sometimes I can get it. But I realize how helpless and far away I am from recovery—or whatever it is! (laughs) Recovery or—

Jay: Whatever it is! (Frank continues to laugh) Whatever it is all of us are doing! (extended laughter) We can get pretty serious about whatever it is we're doing! (laughter)

Frank: I've been here what, almost five, six weeks, Jesus! I guess I thought five or six weeks ago in five or six weeks at least I'd be comfortable. I can't believe that I'd thought I'd be like I am now. And yet, I don't think I could believe that I'd be walking. (laughs)

Jay: Yes.

Frank: I couldn't believe I'd be as far behind, whatever that means, and I couldn't believe I'd be that far ahead. (laughs)

Jay: Part of the pain comes from the expectations of where you're supposed to be.

Frank: And, also, part of the exhilaration.

PATIENT-SCHOLAR – JAY

infirm,
he calls
himself
to action
as he'd played squash,
nothing
held back

despite
pain,
medication,
dependence
he challenges
hospital policy
values
free parking
for visitors,
nurses' humor

not
your docile
patient:
would he
ditch

lifetime habits
just for
catastrophe?

he seeks
to understand
the institution
enclosing him

what debates
inform
his treatment

why is
his body's chaos
mirrored
by the hospital's?

how
might the
hospital behemoth
be forced
to change
its course

he goes inward
disclosing
drug-caused
confusion
about
the country
where he lives,
desires
to entertain
his friends

Jay Clark and Aura Sanchez Garfunkel

so they'll
keep visiting

voices
despair
over
endless battles
with the hospital,
affection
for those
who
feed,
bathe
and dress him

I am drawn
to this man's
fight
to be a person,
not
just
a
patient

already one
who spoke his mind
before his injury
Frank keeps
that feistiness

I never know
what we'll explore
together,
what's occurred
to him

in intervening days,
whether he'll be
up or down
in spirit

only
that
we'll talk
in depth—
our means
of travel

for all
his pain,
frustration,
broken dreams,
adventure's gleam
lights
our conversations

PART III. THE STRUGGLE INTENSIFIES

In a series of encounters, Frank advocates with the hospital director for better response to patients' needs, copes with a student physical therapist who drops him on the floor, and is refused an aide to help him eat. In tears, Frank speaks of running out of energy to fight the constant battles with hospital staff.

HEIGHTENED AWARENESS - JAY

a sunset seen
a symphony heard
at five in the morning
nurses' care
things of wonder,

wiggle of toes
a publication,
one step
a triumph,
a slip,
a defeat,
the grace
of a physical therapist,
indescribable

muscles stilled
eye sharpened

fortune crossed
life savored

Frank and Jay, Monday, October 19, 1992, Part 1: "A danger in these dialogues"

Frank: What got me thinking was that people come here and suddenly start talking about my arm, my walking, my hands, my butt; and I am as interested in their lives, in your life, as I am in my life. With Aura, I think it's very successful in the sense that she's here a lot and I am finding out a lot about her marvelous experience with this new job [as Director of Human Services in Chelsea, MA]. In a way, it's like me turning from my stomach to my back. She went from DSS [MA Department of Social Services] and the misery of wasted time and frustration, to working in an office where everyone likes her and she likes people. Where she goes around the city and meets people and sees programs. Suddenly she feels that she is part of something. So there is a balance there: I hear a lot about her and she hears a lot about me. I am very conscious when she comes in that I don't want her to just ask how I am. And you shared with me some of the stuff about your teaching. I think that's a very big danger in these dialogues—with you, with anyone. It just becomes focused on me, almost an obsession with, body, pills, and pains. The only thing I can see that doing is making the pain worse!

Jay: Well, I hear what you're saying. I agree with you and I disagree. I disagree to the extent that for all of us who know you and care about you, your ordeal is an ordeal for us, too. In my dreams, my ruminations, your experience enters powerfully, it's true for faculty members, it's true for a lot of your friends. Our experiences are about you; that is, not exclusively so, but powerfully so. You know, I ride my bike over to Cambridge; and there was an article in the Globe today about some other fellow who fell off his bike and snapped his head back. I was thinking, 'Jesus, I've been doing that for about 20 years.

Frank: Without a helmet. (laughs)

Jay: Without a helmet and with potholes. I've fallen off my bike, I've been hit by 2 cars, I run into several cars myself (Frank laughs) and I've hit the MBTA tracks and gone over head-over-heels—you know, when you get your wheels stuck in the rails.

Frank: And so have I. (laughs)

Jay: And Kitty goes out every day and rides on the bike. She adjusts my seat because her bike was stolen. Hops on the bike.

Frank: Without a helmet.

Jay: Without a helmet.

Frank: But you're very careful about eating the right things (laughter) and you don't smoke.

Jay: That's part of the irony of life, that it will tumble someone when they have taken the greatest care. This guy was wearing a helmet, by the way, when he had the accident; it didn't make a bit of difference. So, that's part of my experience with you. A lot of very intriguing things are going on in my life at the moment. How can I say this? It isn't that I come in and focus on you. It's that your story draws me in. There is some very intense, powerful stuff going on for you with this walking, with these encounters with the nurse, and with the system.

Frank: I'd like to think that these encounters have that universal characteristic, and I see them in those terms. I could see them in my ordinary life, but they're so vivid now. The colors are so sharp and the sounds are often so wrenching. Or in some cases so beautiful. The Natashas of the world or the Jackies of the world, [two nurses], and sitting in that room and seeing that sunset and listening to the Beethoven Seventh at five o'clock in the morning. It's just like, I guess like, they say LSD is.

Jay: Yes, I was going to say, a trip.

Frank: A trip that seems to go on and on. And a new installment today (laughs).

It started Saturday. I got this new physical therapist, who I got to know the first few days I came in here; and then, except for seeing her around, I haven't had any contacts with her. Her name is Teresa. So I'm doing this walking with her and Aura is videotaping. This is the fourth day that I've walked. The first three days I was *struggling*, trying to pick up my feet, rather than just flowing. On this fourth day, Teresa says, "Look I'm new to you and I don't know if this is going to work or not." Suddenly my body learns how to walk; my body starts walking. And Aura is filming, and I'm just ecstatic because I'm not struggling anymore; I'm not trying to pick my feet up, which is not what you do in this kind of walking. Somewhere along the line, Aura asks Teresa whether she's familiar with—what is it, Feldinghouse?

Jay: Feldenkreis.

Frank: —whether she is familiar with Feldenkreis, and she lights up and says, "Yes, I've been studying and I'm taking a seminar in Montreal." And so Aura has read all about Feldenkreis and they immediately find themselves in great harmony with each other. And although I don't know Feldenkreis—

Jay: A very gentle approach—

Frank: —it turns out that I know a lot about Feldenkreis, but I didn't know it by name. I would have called it an approach to movement.

So, that was Saturday. Sunday I don't have any physical therapy. Today was such a gigantic day, with Anelisa going through oral surgery and me breaking down any number of times just trying to deal with it. And Anelisa coming over last night, and my saying "You'll have to talk a lot today because you're not going to talk for the next six weeks." Then her hugging me and crying; me going through the night, looking at the clock and knowing when she was going to be in the hospital and when she was going into the operating room.

Jay: She went in the hospital this morning?

Frank: Six o'clock this morning. She was in the operating room four hours. Then Aura comes to me —Al is here— about one o'clock, and tells me that it was successful and that Anelisa's okay, she's in the recovery room; we just hugged each other, and I felt how much of a burden it was on both of us.

At three o'clock I went back to the computer room by myself because I had an hour of open time, and lost track of the time. I met some people down there—some staff who were interested in me—and I was late to physical therapy.

Teresa says: "Well, I don't want to make an issue of it, but I was waiting for you and in the future"... So I blew up at her. "Do you know what I've been doing for the last five months [sic] in this hospital? Do you know that I sat around waiting while my feet would die before the nurses would come, and I waited for physical therapists and occupational therapists? Therapists have changed their times with me at the last minute, when I had other plans!" So we had it out!

Sue [a former student] was here. Ordinarily, when I go to physical therapy, if there's is one visitor around they stay. So I said, "Teresa, would it be ok if Sue stuck around?" And Teresa said, "No, it would not be." I couldn't really talk to anyone, and I didn't know what she had in mind so we kind of agreed to drop it.

Then she proceeded to pull the room divider and close the door of the therapy room, and that was weird; no one has ever done that before. She told me that she had been studying Feldenkreis. She was new at it; she had taken the course and she had the book right there, and she said, "I'd like to try it out." She introduced it by saying that it involved very minute stuff, very careful, slow stuff, and that you needed to become very conscious of your movements and your rhythm and things like that.

I liked what she said. I didn't like the fact that she didn't introduce what she was doing before she shut the door. And I didn't know if she shut the door because she didn't want everyone else to see what she was doing, since it was pretty radical. At one point she said, "This is physical therapy," but I suspect it's really not. I said, "Okay. So far so good; my wife certainly is into it, and really likes that way of thinking about the body and movement and the mind." Then she proceeded to do it almost right from the book. She had me get on my back and lift my legs up and shut my eyes.

Jay: Just the right day for it—

Frank: —with Anelisa and my arm, my meeting with my doctor, who had been gone for two weeks! So, anyway, we started doing this stuff, the Feldenkreis physical therapy— as you say, it was an extraordinary day to do it—and it was extremely relaxing: Teresa told me, "You really are the right person for this. I really think this technique is right, but none of these other patients could do this, unless they learned a lot about doing it from someone like me." I said, "I feel the same way about you. I had an experience with you the first weekend I was here which was very memorable and I was sorry you weren't the therapist I had." And then we had this rare experience on Saturday with the walking.

Jay: It's a third example of your having a fight with someone and then a marvelous experience.

Frank: (laughs) That's right. You've known me in my personal relationships (laughs) and my medical relationships.

Jay: A Garfunklian approach to progress. You all right? Do you want the pillow plumped up a bit? It's sliding off.

Frank: You know what I'd like to do; I'd like to put my feet up; see if you could block them with something. I want to put them really up. Take that foot stand and put it at the end of the bed.

(Jay elevates Frank's feet with the foot stand) So, at the end of the time we were both kind of —

Jay: —mellow—

Frank: —mellow and appreciative of the fact that we were going to do this together and that she was going to give me an article to read. Then Aura came on the scene and Teresa bumped into Aura. They got into almost an hour-long conversation, really getting into what Feldenkreis was about and what she was doing. Aura also wanted to know what she thought about acupuncture for my shoulder, and would this hospital be receptive to it. Teresa doubted it but suggested that we might ask. It really ended up on a good note.

MENTOR - JAY

I nursed
obstruction
as a child

when mother
taught me how
to write
I gnarled the letters,
miss-spelt the words,
but kept defiance
wordless

when I was four
father
tested me for smarts:
close the window, remove the pencil from the drawer
and put the paper on the desk
I said no

he went to mother,
gently told her
not to hope
for my success

through years of schooling
I learned to speak
and write
my thoughts
but kept
contrary ones
at home

something
in me
sought
and feared
a row

and so I often
walked
the road around
instead of
going up against

but then
I took a job
with Frank
as boss

to my delight,
I found
him skilled
in oppositional arts

authority's decisions
institutions' policies
tradition's laws
curriculum's design,
colleagues' thinking

academia's values:

he took them on—
observed, queried,
reasoned, declaimed
mocked, disdained.

whom I had met
with gritted teeth
he disarmed with
quick repartee
easy humor
raffish antics:

I rejoiced
when he strode
into the dean's office,
snatched the ceremonial trowel
that laid the school's last stone

as if to run him through
he thrust it at the dean
who smiled wanly,
his academic dignity
tumbled

such ease
encouraged
openness
about my
odds
with others

in years with Frank
I learned

to draw
opposing
outwards
see and speak it
not with his bravado
but with my own desire
for conversation
and a meeting
of minds

FRANK AND JAY, MONDAY, OCTOBER 19, 1992, PART 2: "I'M FINDING OUT THAT IT'S ALMOST IMPOSSIBLE TO TELL PEOPLE CERTAIN THINGS"

Frank: I think my big problem really is with my body relearning; my mind is going to enter into it too. At one point I told a therapist, "Stop telling me to pull my butt in while standing or walking, just hit my butt." And she said, "Okay". Every time she wanted me to put my butt in, instead of saying it, she just tapped it. It was kind of interesting: I was much more responsive to the kinesthetic message than I was to the verbal message. I told Teresa that, because she kept on saying, "Let your mind think of what it is like."

One of the things you are supposed to do is curl up your spine so that there is a little hole that a mouse could run through. She said, "With your eyes shut, visualize and then try and do it. Let the visualization and the trying to do it begin to merge." One of the other things is to go from one side to the other and realize what happens to your shoulders, what happens to your head, what happens to your feet, what's happening to your body, when you go through a simple thing like doing this. (gestures) You are visualizing it and you are doing it and trying to integrate that. It's a question of the integrity of the movements of the mind.

I've always realized that that's what this is all about. Muscle training and muscle strengthening are going to come because I'm going to get stuff back and I'm going to exercise. But that doesn't guarantee that the stuff will become integrated. Teresa's work with Feldenkreis seems to create a very small and explicit way to integrate different movements. So I'm kind of on my way; I'll do a little reading.

Jay: Did she move your arms too?

Frank: She was having me move my hips to make a tunnel, to go right, to go left, to go down to 12 o'clock, up to 6 o'clock, 3 o'clock, 9 o'clock. I am sure there are other dimensions that involve your arms in very explicit ways. She said in the end, "I'm trying to teach you and I'm trying to learn from you".

Jay: She sounds like a remarkable person.

Frank: She is. When you compare her to all the other therapists here, they're nice, they're kids. Typically, when I ask them, as we talked about before, "What're the controversies in your field?" They don't know. She knows. She knows enough to shut all the doors when she tries that stuff out (laughs). A little bit deceptive on our part to do it that way. She could have told me, "Look, this is pretty far out stuff, do you want to do it? I'm going to have to shut the doors." Of course that could make her liable.

Jay: I think you have to be pretty paranoid; when you're a member of a profession you've got to watch your ass. Any profession.

Frank: But she also has to be concerned about doing it with me. Because I'm not exactly a hayseed.

Jay: But she got some message—

Frank: —she got a message from Aura—

Jay: —and a message from you.

Frank: And, in a way, a message from me, yeah. But I must say, it was weird the way the whole thing unfolded.

Jay: It sounds like a remarkable experience and a breakthrough. … Your legs all right? You got a cramp?

Frank: No. Are they shaking?

Jay: They were shaking; they're not shaking now. Somehow, if you had access to that position [feet braced against a box] in the middle of the night when you got a cramp, you could get rid of it.

Frank: Yeah, that's true. But I don't. (laughs) Of course I do move around a lot and bring my legs up. But if I go on my side or I cross my legs or anything like that, I'm going to get cramps. I want to do those things, but I don't want to get cramps. When I press to relieve the cramp, that's not doing anything. When I relax—

Jay: —I assume she would have you press very slowly and relax very slowly and feel the whole business.

Frank: Yeah, right, that's right.

Jay: That's very Eastern. It's meditative, the notion of doing something very slowly. The Japanese Tea Ceremony is done with extreme carefulness and precision, being aware of every muscle of your body as you reach out to pour the tea.

(conversation continues as tape is changed)

Frank: What was I saying?

Jay: There were two assistants at your physical therapy session.

Frank: Oh, yeah. They're both young. One is a graduate of the University of Colorado in kineasthesiology and is going to study physical therapy. The other is a student of physical therapy at Northeastern. They are both really nice. (**Nurse comes in and gives Frank his medications and she and Jay adjust Frank for the night.**)

Among other things, the assistants both exercise my legs. They do it by taking my ankles, bending the legs up, lifting the legs up, stretching the hamstrings, taking them out to the side. They both do the same thing and they both do it very slowly and they do it in entirely different ways. Sally, from Northeastern, does it and it's nice. Fran, the young lady from Colorado, is a Zen artist. When she does the same thing, it's just entirely different. So one day Paula [a colleague] was here with her husband. She's a good observer and we have had lots of good talks about things. I told her, "You might want to observe this, because I think it's just totally unique." So Paula observed, and she too just stared for thirty-five or forty minutes while this woman did this beautiful stuff with my legs. Like you said, it's slow and it's got certain characteristics; but it has other characteristics that are really not describable.

Jay: If one really gets into it, it's a meditation; Buddhists teach a walking meditation: first you put your heel down and then the ball of your foot and toe. If you're doing it right, you are just completely wrapped up in the movements of your body when you walk. Then, when you sit and meditate, you are wrapped up in your breathing and completely aware of your posture and breathing.

It's not easy to attain that and keep it. I can't keep it for very long. But, for moments when I do, it's very powerful and very integrative.

(Frank asks to use the urinal and instructs Jay on how set things up. Jay notices that Frank uses his hands to move himself in his bed)

Jay: You're really moving your fingers more.

Frank: Well, they feel really stiff, but I think I'm just learning to use what I have better. You see, I can do a lot more with this thumb.

Jay: When Teresa does the Feldenkreis, does she do stuff with your hands?

Frank: No, not yet, the only thing we worked on is that one position.

Jay: Are you getting massage for your hands every day?

Frank: There is one therapist that usually massages them, but I don't have her every day. Massage is just not part of the operation here. The massages I've gotten were from some of the people that come here, from Al, you and Aura. I think it should be part of the program.

Jay: Should your arm be in this sling here? (he struggles to arrange the splint) You'd think after ten times I'd know which direction to go in. But motor learning has never been one of my strong points.

Frank: If you wanted to see something funny, you should have been there when [a visitor] and I tried to set up the computer. We had some time together and I said, "Well, I need to set up a student's dissertation and a proposal on the computer." He said "Fine".

So we went down to the computer and I turned it on. I got the thing going and then I took a look at the documents. One of them was set up in such a way that I had to change the setup to read it. I had to increase the margins, which with a mouse and my two hands would have taken me all of five seconds. You've never used a Macintosh have you? It takes about three seconds to shade the document, a second to change the margin, and less than a second to hit return.

But in order for me to do it without a mouse, first I had to shade it; I discovered how to do that. Then I had to change the margins without the mouse, and I finally discovered how to do that. In the meantime I inadvertently pressed the wrong key with my bumbling hands and erased the whole chapter.

Jay: Jesus!

Frank: I eventually did undo that and I got it back. So I said to him "Let's try another chapter and I'm going to need your help". He said, "Okay, what shall I do?" I guess you're not going to appreciate how funny this is, not being a Mac user, but I tried, in words, to tell him what to do and I could not get him to do it.

He moved the mouse down and said, "There's no more room to move it." I said, "Just pick it up and move it down again." (Jay laughs) and he couldn't understand that. He started moving something down and I said, "Well, keep it going," so he goes up the computer...(laughter) it was like I was dealing with someone with Down's Syndrome and trying to teach him integral calculus. It was hysterical. He just couldn't get it. And he wanted to in the worst way.

I'm finding out it's almost impossible to tell people certain things. Like I've tried to explain to people how to put my hand on the phone so I can talk to someone. I've tried it dozens of times now, and unless they see it, everyone tries to get me to hold the phone in some way—with my arm perpendicular to the phone— like everyone holds the phone. I say no, it's not perpendicular, it's parallel to the phone. They can't understand; it just doesn't make any sense. I haven't developed a language to explain that. It's the same with explaining to someone how to use a mouse.

FRANK AND JAY, MONDAY, OCTOBER 26, 1992: "AS WE LEARN TOGETHER, WE ARE LEARNING HOW TO LEARN"

Frank: On Friday, we didn't walk at all, but the physical therapist did some very interesting things with me, having me stand up and get balance. Interestingly enough, when she did it she said, "Well, I know that this is what *you* want to do"—

Jay: —yes, without the braces—

Frank: —she didn't say it with any acrimony or anything. She just said, "I want to work with you on the mat, but I know you want to stand up every day." And it's true.

On Saturday, the mirror was down in front of me and I was walking and having a really bad time of it. Suddenly it occurred to me that everything the therapists were telling me was lateral, not frontal. In order to identify the corrections you had to be at my side, not my front; and yet, the mirror was in front of me. They said, "Push your butt in," and you could only see that from the side; then they said something about the knees, that's side; they said something about my chest. It finally hit me.

I said, "Why don't you put the mirror on my side, because everything you tell me is lateral." They put it on my side, and suddenly I started walking. Everything they said made sense. When they said "Stop piking" [bending the hips and leaning forward], I could see myself piking and I would react immediately.

114

I thought it was an interesting metaphor for teaching and learning; it's essential that the cues we use are really appropriate for the learning that is going on.

Jay: That we stay in our own orientation.

Frank: Yeah, that lateral orientation. That's somewhat similar to how I had the therapist hit me on the butt rather than tell me. As we learn together, we are learning how to learn and what the cues are, where they should come from and how they should be made. Today I continued walking and it was extremely successful. My legs started doing what I wanted them to do and my body started doing what I wanted it to do.

Jay: If the therapists send you the right messages in an orientation you can use, that makes it easier for you to send, and receive, perhaps, some kind of messages in your legs. But if they don't give you the right messages, you can't send your legs the right messages.

Frank: It's that old disjointedness we talked about before, between the different parts of my body. In a sense the balance is the integrity: it's bringing together of the whole thing and we call it balance. When you think about it, what is balance? It's integration. It's pulling all those things together. And that goes for a lot of different kinds of balance—the balance of one's psychological functions, family balance—

Jay: It's interesting, I was meeting today with a colleague and we had this see-saw. We were getting ready to do a workshop on balancing family demands and work demands. If the see-saw is in perfect balance, it is not dynamic. You need a constant flow of information about what is happening in order to keep one set of demands from overwhelming the other. Often, the problem is, you're getting some information, but you're not getting all the feedback you need to stay in balance, since it's a dynamic act, not static.

Frank: The balance comes about because all this information is coordinated or synchronized. I don't know what the right word is.

Jay: It's like your legs are giving you some information and your rear end is giving you too much.

Frank: Well, the muscles in the rear end, the gluteus maximus, they are just not developed enough for me to really walk yet. I can pick myself up, but once I get up, I really don't have a sense of how to stay up. The different parts of my system, the foot system, the butt system, and the knee system, they just don't go together yet.

So, it's very humbling, since I'm continually focusing on what it's going to take for me to get out of this place. I asked the doctor today what her estimate now was, and she said it was eight weeks from now, bringing us to the end of December—which I found difficult, but realistic, probably.

Jay: Does she also say the things you need to be able to do before you can get out of here?

Frank: Well, no.

Jay: That would be helpful if she did.

Frank: I've discussed that quite a bit with the psychiatrist; he's the one who is interested in knowing what I think I need to get out of here. Today, we spent an hour talking about walking into my house and being able to go to the bathroom, being able to transfer myself to a wheelchair or to a car. I'm quite a ways away from that, even with my standing up and all the other strengths I have.

She says that when I get home, I'll have another half of my rehabilitation to go and I understand that. But that will be very significant—when I get home.

Jay: Sure! Jesus! (Frank chuckles) Just being home itself will do something. At that point could you get some out-patient treatment?

Frank: The chances are that I'll continue my program with the hospital. They will send someone out to the house and, as soon as I become more mobile, I will be coming in here on a regular basis. So, I'm talking about the therapist coming to my house every single day. I'll be getting the same amount of therapy I'm getting here.

Jay: You should.

Frank: The psychiatrist asked, "What will your home be like?" I said, "Well, I can control my home, I can have shelves, I can have a telephone situation that works; I can have switches that work. I can engineer my home so that I can be comfortable and independent, no matter what stage I'm at."

Jay: Maybe you could set up a daily schedule in terms of meeting with students, reading or whatever you want to do; you won't have the interruptions you have here.

Frank: Plus I can call in and call out. I can have an answering machine, have people around. Seems like a dream world! (laughter) A fucking Garden of Eden you know! Jesus!

Now Anelisa is home [from her stay in the hospital following oral surgery], and looking really well. I talked to Aura on the phone and Anelisa was out in the car and I almost died. I said, "Aura, she just went through major surgery, she went through major anesthesia, and she's still under medication!—"

Jay: —she's got your genes Frank!—

Frank: "—and you've let her out in the goddamn car!"

Jay: You would have been out there too!

Frank: I couldn't believe she'd be out there.

Jay: You will be out there too! (laughter) Driving around with your hands or something or other, your feet! (laughter)

Frank: My penis! (laughter) My feet are on the steering wheel! (laughter)

Jay: You'll get pulled over for indecent driving!

Frank: Another incident that I thought we'd mention, too, is an encounter with the director of the hospital. Nancy [a friend] was over here yesterday. We were walking around the hospital talking and I stopped in to say hello to another patient. She went into the solarium at the other end of the building and ran into this guy who was taking notes. She, being a very gregarious person, started talking to him.

He asked who she was visiting and she said, "Professor Garfunkel." And he said, "Well, how's he doing?" And she said—which was the key to the whole encounter—"Well, I think you ought to ask him." (laughter) Rather than saying, "You know, he's doing fine." He was cornered. He had to ask me. So then I came in and he asked me how I was doing.

Jay: But you didn't know who he was at this point.

Frank: No, I can't remember when I found out, but it was pretty quick. I said that I thought it was a very fine place with a lot of good staff, a lot of caring people. "But, you can put a light on and wait an hour and it does kind of dwell on your dependency rather than your independency." He seemed to be interested, but with a poker face. When I told him about the incident you and I had [when no one responded to Frank's having pressed the buzzer for help], he didn't seem to show anything on his face. We talked for about 30 minutes—I talked about the computer situation, about the staffing situation; I didn't bring up everything I had observed, obviously—but I couldn't tell if he was interested.

Jay: He kept his 'poker demeanor'.

Frank: The aftermath was that he went to the nurses' station and started inquiring about how and when patient calls were answered, and he asked all kinds of questions. That night, whenever I rang the nurses' bell, I got a reply in less than two minutes. (laughter) All the nurses knew that I had spoken to him. Every shift, it went around—

Jay: —that's how the system works—

Frank: —and then he asked me to write a letter to him, which I planned to do; my stenographer came in tonight, but she got all tied up and was getting me something to eat, and other people came in, so I didn't write the letter. But he was very responsive. And the nurses said, "Yeah, the only people they listen to are patients." Which is interesting. (laughter)

Jay: I guess you might say he's purifying the system around here. If he's coming in on Sunday, there might be some bullets he's trying to dodge.

Frank: He's a workaholic, they tell me. He works seven days a week. Totally dedicated to the hospital. He sees some patients, even though he's the general director of the place.

Then nurses started coming up to me, asking, "What did you tell him?" And there are two explanations for the problem: one is that the staff is not competent and is dogging it, and not answering the buttons; the other is, there's not enough staff. The director seems to take the former explanation. I think they're both true.

Jay: Well, you goose the system and it's always going to respond. Any system will respond like that.

Frank: When Theresa [a nurse] came to see me, she said, "What did you tell him about me?" I said, "Look, I told him that you were terrific and that you should be paid by the pound!" (laughter) She got a big kick out of that; she thought that was very funny. (laughter)

Jay: They probably appreciate the fact that you talked with him; they must have concerns too.

Frank: The question is, are they competent in what they do, and do they follow up on when patients call them? I think there is a certain amount of incompetence, a certain amount of "Oh, another call from that patient who's always complaining". There has to be a mentality that "When a patient rings or calls us, we have got to look at it, we've got to pay attention to it, do something about it". Last night they certainly didn't keep me waiting at all.

I think they need data: they need a system where, when a light goes on, it gets recorded some place; and when the light is answered, they know what the average lag time is—how many times it's over twenty minutes, how many times it's over forty minutes, and how many times it's over an hour. I think of the 911 system; every time a call is made it's recorded, and how long it takes for response is recorded. Maybe that's what they need here.

Jay: There must be equipment that would be fairly easy to plug into to get that.

Frank: Oh, I would think so, but that would mean an expenditure of money.

Jay: Well, if he really wants to know—

Frank: —then that's the way to find out.

Jay: A lot of those people are helpless with their board of trustees, until they get a complaint like this. In that sense you have more power than any physician or even the director.

Frank: Depending on how I communicate it. In my letter, I'll mention that he needs better data. I'll tell him a lot of calls are answered promptly, but a lot are not, particularly between 6:30 and 7:30 in the morning, when the shifts are changing. (**Frank periodically drifts off to sleep for a few moments and then returns to his topic**) Another issue I cited was the computers and where they're placed: how they can be better used. The third issue was patients coming in and not really having vocational goals while they are here. … Let's say they bring someone in to teach patients how to use some software. If they have a bunch of computers and a bunch of people all together. … There's a better way to get organized, better than sticking a computer on every floor.

I also want to mention the issue of involving the patient in planning what happens to them. Today my occupational therapist announced that they were going to sit me in the hallway for lunch. I'd eat on my own, and if I needed help a nurse would come and help me.

I really blew up at that. "If you're planning to change, why don't you ask me and see what I have to say about it." And she said, "We just don't have enough personnel to feed you separately." I said, "Well, let's talk about it, what it involves. Can I really eat on my own in the hall? Do I want to eat in the hall?" Pretty grim, eating in the hall, lined up with some of the people that are lined up there.

I told her in no uncertain terms that I would not eat lunch if I have to eat in the hall. So that was a pretty tense lunch we had today. Not in the hall, in my room.

Jay: Yeah, that sounds grim; that's out of Burt's *Christmas In Purgatory* [A book by Burton Blatt, Frank's mentor and former chairman of the Special Education Department, exposing living conditions within state institutions for the mentally retarded].

Frank: They claim that they have to do it to save staff time. In my case, between the time that you and others give here, and the time Aura has given, and Gail [a friend] assisting Frank at nights], we've provided hundreds of hours of staff time; and they can't provide fifteen or twenty minutes for someone to help me eat in my room? In the privacy of my room? It just doesn't make any sense.

Jay: (taking notes) Do you want to include in your letter the psychiatrist's statement that you ought to be a member of the team?

Frank: I'm going to say that I have had some support from staff here, but patients should be involved in the planning— it's better for their treatment. The fact that very little of it is done here and very little time is taken is an indication that this place is not really up to current thinking on treatment.

These are systemic issues. If they really think patient contribution is important, they'll make time for it. They don't even have time for the treatment team to get together; the psychiatrist just meets with people individually. There's little evidence of people getting together as a total team and talking about issues—like the issue of where someone should eat.

I talked to the doctor today and mentioned that I had an OT over the weekend who, I thought, was very interesting in the way she handled my arm. The doctor simply wasn't interested; she said, "Oh, those OT's, they have all kinds of tricks, but the important thing is that your body gets ready to have new behaviors, new senses." She totally rejected what those people were doing: "So, it's OK; just let them do it; let them kind of help out and exercise you."

She rejects it because she thinks they should keep my limbs stretched, extended and make sure that they don't lock into place.

My aim was to get her to assign that therapist to me on a regular basis, but she obviously wasn't about to do that.

Jay: It's really a crisis intervention response rather than a developmental response. Would that be fair to say?

Frank: (after a period of sleep) I don't know how much I should say about all these issues.

Jay: I'll put these things down and you can review it tomorrow.

Frank: It's one thing to make some recommendations that they can incorporate, like keeping track of responses to the buzzer. It's another thing to challenge the hierarchy, challenge how they do business. In a way, I think that's the more important thing, to challenge how they do business, but I don't know how you do that or when you do that. … How long have I been on my back?

Jay: You've been there for thirty-five minutes. If you like, I'll give you a massage before you're turned over.

Frank: Yeah, why don't you do that. … I don't know whether you want to keep the tape on. Just to get my groans!

Jay: (laughs) Okay, I'll turn it off.

Frank: My ecstasy!

Jay: This is not true research, because we're eliminating Frank's groans from the body of data!

A LIFE UNBOUND: THE EARLY YEARS (1927-1957) - AURA

In 1922, Eva Garfunkel, a trim, no-nonsense twenty-four year-old, was employed as a home care nurse to assist a six year old child who was ill with pneumonia. The child, Celeste, was the niece of a thirty-seven year old Jewish Viennese émigré by the name of Henry Garfunkel. Henry had come to the United States with five older brothers when he was a teenager. Eva and Henry's instant attraction to each other was no doubt hastened by the fact that they shared the same last name, although their families had emigrated from different parts of Eastern Europe. Eva's parents were orthodox Jews who had come from Poland to New Jersey, where she was born, the eldest of four. Both families were fairly well off. On June 14, 1925, Eva and Henry married, honeymooned at Yellowstone and settled in Jersey City, N.J. Their daughter Charlotte was born on July 11, 1926 and their son Frank on November 17, 1927.

After Henry died in 1950, Eva had a few serious suitors, but none could ever measure up to Henry, and thus she chose not to remarry. There was only one man, Eva said, who would ever be her husband, and that was Henry. In later years, Frank would not hesitate to remind her, half in jest and half seriously, that her rosy view of the marriage relationship was revisionist history; Henry could be difficult and demanding, expecting things to be done his way. Understandably, Eva would get furious at Frank. "What do you know?" she'd say defensively. "What ever happened to you?" she'd continue, attributing Frank's cutting remark to a character defect he had undoubtedly acquired after leaving the civility of her home. "You used to be such a sweet boy." Despite Eva's strong temperament, it was Henry, according to Frank, who ruled the roost. Their arguments and her frustrations had not been lost on the children. Frank was the only one who dared to tease Eva or stand up to her; mother and son had a close bond. She'd get angry, but clearly adored him and forgave him his 'disrespect,' while Frank had the utmost admiration for his mother's strength and spunk.

Charlotte remembers her mother as always doting on Frank. He was a quiet child who, she says, was introspective - "into himself." Small for his age, with light brown curly hair and hazel eyes, he closely resembled his mother and would eventually develop Eva's iron will and independent streak. When he was about one and a half years old, he had to have a double mastoid operation, and would endure numerous, painful ear infections. At four he was afflicted by polio, the dreaded disease that struck fear into the heart of every parent during the 30s, 40s and 50s. Against the strong advice of the family doctor and the prevailing views of the time, Eva courageously and in desperation opted to treat Frank in accordance with the controversial Sister Kenny method. This involved applying hot packs to the affected muscles to keep them relaxed. Eva continued to massage Frank's weak muscles months after his illness had subsided. Perhaps as a result of this treatment, Frank escaped the ravages of the dreaded disease with only a weak eye muscle and an almost undetectable limp. Because of the fear of contagion, five-year-old Charlotte was required to live with her grandmother Esther, Aunts Kay and Freda and Uncle Jack in Mount Vernon, NY for a number of months. She remembers it as a confusing but enjoyable time, where her relatives treated her as if she were a princess.

In later years, Eva would say that Frank, despite his many stressful maladies, was the best baby ever, never complaining or crying no matter how much suffering he was subjected to. Charlotte however, remembers her little brother not so much for his bravery or endurance as for being a pest, forever tagging behind her and her friends, forcing her to devise creative strategies for ditching him. Once, she locked him in an ambulance when the drivers left the doors ajar while they went in to attend to an emergency call from a neighbor. Eventually he was set free by the returning drivers. For a long time, Charlotte carried great guilt over this incident. In later years, she forced herself to apologize to her brother for the misdeed, only to learn that he had no memory of it.

When Frank was four, the family moved from Jersey City to Palisades. Henry now had a longer work commute, having kept the electrical business that he owned with his five brothers, in Jersey City. The family rented several homes in the area. The first was a large home with orchards, a maid and a butler. When the Depression came, Henry's business went bankrupt and the family had to move to a smaller house. (Despite this misfortune, Henry went on to start another highly successful electrical business.) It is unclear why Eva and Henry decided to move their family from their comfortable, predominantly Jewish neighborhood in Jersey City to Palisades, a community devoid of Jews. Whatever the reasons, the move had negative effects on both children. Being the only Jews in their classes made it difficult for them to fit in and make friends. They were taunted and ridiculed. Charlotte remembers feeling different: "I tried hard to get kids to like me." Frank recollected that it was an isolating experience where he was punished for being Jewish and different.

During these early school-age years, Frank not only had to tolerate illnesses and prejudice, but was also plagued by learning difficulties. He was left-handed, in a school that adhered to the Palmer method of penmanship, and had no tolerance for left-handed writing. As a result, his writing was indecipherable. He was forced to sit apart from the other students in the class, labeled a student with learning problems. Charlotte remembers that "even as a youngster, I thought they were being cruel to Frank, making him write with his right hand." After consulting mental health professionals, who told her that the school should simply allow him to write with his left hand, Eva succeeded in getting the school not to segregate Frank and to give up on the hand switch. Perhaps these early episodes with being 'different' and set apart from other youngsters laid the foundation for his eventual dedication to the rights of another marginalized people: the disabled.

Although only a year older, Charlotte was almost twice Frank's size by the time they were in grade school. She suggests that perhaps "because of his size, he went out for sports in a great way. He love[d] sports and he was really good at them." He played ice hockey, and football and was involved in wrestling. (It was not until his later teen years that Frank caught up to Charlotte in size.) When Frank was twelve, Henry had his first heart attack. Frank was away at camp, while Charlotte was home and required to help with her father's care. Eva successfully nursed Henry back to health.

As a businessman in the hurly-burly of Jersey City, Henry was active in the machinery of the Democratic Party and played high-stakes poker with some of the party regulars, including some of Mayor Haig's cronies. A round-faced man with warm brown eyes, Henry had only gone as far as the sixth grade. He was intelligent, with an especially sharp mind for business - and card playing, which helped to supplement the family's income.

When Frank was sixteen, Henry had another mild heart attack, causing the family to move back to Jersey City to lessen the stress of commuting. Frank finished high school in 1943, at Stevens Hoboken Academy. Now a young adult giving more thought to his future, he made clear to his father that despite the success of the family business, he had no intention of making that his career. Henry was angry and intolerant of Frank's decision. Charlotte remembers how upset her father was, and ironically, how she would have jumped at the chance that her brother was so determined to reject. Gender roles and expectations weighed heavily on both the son and the daughter. She liked the world of business. "[I] would have loved to have gone into the business, but no one ever asked me." It was inconceivable to her at the time, she recalls, that she could have replaced Frank as the company heir. (Long after her children were grown, Charlotte entered the work world and had much success working as a bookkeeper with the Nature Conservancy in Concord, New Hampshire.)

For Charlotte, both Henry and Eva could be a bit intimidating. Eva could be wrathful and domineering. Many years later, I too would come to experience Eva's difficult and overbearing personality. Early in our marriage, not at all happy that Frank and I had married, she warned me that her son had been hurt before in his first two marriages and that I must not hurt him again. I was furious at her for what I saw as meddling. It was only when I had sons of my own that I came to understand her need to protect hers: to understand how difficult it is to sit by the sidelines and see the hurts and frustrations our children inevitably experience in the process of living their lives.

Charlotte was convinced that as far as Eva was concerned, Frank was the favored child, and why not? Didn't he also physically resemble Eva and share the same take-charge characteristics? But perhaps it was simply that he was the younger, and had been beset with so many childhood ailments, so that Eva may have felt she had to be more protective of him. Although a gentle man, Henry had a rather distant relationship with both children. Charlotte didn't so much fear him as wish he would pay more attention to her. He could be caustic and dismissive. She remembers once bringing home a school paper in which she received an A+. She showed it to her father, whose response was: "Who wrote this for you? Who did you copy it from?" She was devastated by his reaction.

Unlike Charlotte, Frank did not remember his parents as intimidating. Frank was especially close to Eva, and many years later would reflect that it was as if he and Charlotte had been raised by 2 different sets of parents. Despite these different ways of seeing the world of their family, once Charlotte and Frank reached their teens, they became very close. No longer the pesky little brother trailing after her, Frank became a guardian and confidante to Charlotte. She would consult him about boys she was dating, accepting his approval or disapproval of them. She came to realize that she felt closer to Frank than she did to either parent.

In 1945, after finishing high school, Frank enrolled at the University of Michigan where he excelled in sports. Ice hockey was a favorite but he also went out for wrestling. He did not do well academically those first few years and took a leave to join the Marines. During that time, there was virulent anti-Semitism within the Marines. Frank's nose was broken twice because he refused to answer to roll call when his name was, according to Frank, purposely botched up. He could be stubborn and intolerant. Charlotte remembers that at the time she thought he was absolutely crazy to have joined, but attributes his signing up to a fiercely independent and challenging streak that had been developing in Frank since childhood and would continue to define him until his death. Despite the harassment he fulfilled his military assignment in South Carolina and was honorably discharged.

Two years after his discharge, Frank returned to the University of Michigan. His stint in the Marines opened Frank's eyes to the value of a college education. He became especially interested in journalism and the power it had to influence perceptions and expose 'inconvenient' stories to the public. He began to take a greater interest in academics. He completed his course of study with G.I. bill assistance, and graduated in 1949 with a degree in Journalism. After Frank's graduation, the family decided to take a celebratory trip in Frank's car from Ann Arbor to LA. In Minnesota, Henry had another mild heart attack and he and Eva decided to take the train to LA while Frank and Charlotte would continue the drive. They drove via Aspen and were there for the Goethe bi-centennial. They found the event so exciting that they decided to spend a few extra days there, meeting up with friends and attending inspirational lectures. By this time Frank's intellectual and spiritual interests had been greatly stimulated. Charlotte remembers Aspen as a "wonderful experience – we didn't have much money although we both got jobs, so we couldn't afford hotel rooms, and rented one room in a boarding house. I had a difficult time convincing anyone he was only my brother. We stayed longer than we said and [our] parents were very upset with us when we finally reached LA."

Although he had warned his father that he would not go into his business, after college Frank continued to work for his father. His father had opened up the new business with a partner. Once, Frank caught a customer stealing. He confronted the customer and reported it to the partner, who sided with the customer. Frank was infuriated and reported the incident to his father, who was also dismissive of Frank's complaint. He admonished Frank for not minding his own business and told him that the matter would be taken care of; that they dealt with shoplifting customers who were regulars by increasing the price of other paid-for merchandise. There would be no ugly confrontation. The costs of the transgression would just be added on to something else purchased by the customer and the customer would not even know about it. Frank was outraged by his father's unwillingness to confront the matter openly and felt betrayed by his father, his integrity attacked. Henry may have thought that his son had over-reacted – was being over-righteous. The confrontation created an irresolvable rift between the two and a great sadness for Eva. So outraged by his father's reaction was Frank that he abruptly left the job and decided to move out of the family home, keeping occasional contact with his mother.

He headed up to Boston. Soon after arriving, he enrolled in graduate studies in journalism at Boston University (BU), finally on his way to pursuing his own life dreams. Alas, he would come to regret his abrupt departure. Several months later, on November 23, 1950, his father died of a heart attack. There had been no communication with his father since his angry departure and thus, no reconciliation ever took place. Frank deeply regretted that he and Henry never talked about what happened between them. Perhaps Henry too regretted that such a relatively minor matter had caused such a falling out between him and his son. (Coincidently, years later there would be a similar lack of reconciliation between Frank and his first-born son Max.) Frank was distressed at the realization of how he must have hurt his father when he struck out on his own, abandoning the family business. He spent the next couple of years emotionally at a loss, unsure of where to turn or what to do. Years later, whenever he talked to me about his abrupt exodus, it was painfully clear that he wished he could set the clock back and make it right between his father and himself.

A few years before, in Palisades, Frank had met Joan Lovell, the cousin of a friend of his and Charlotte's. They began dating. After the loss of his father, Frank rekindled his relationship with Joan. Joan was the daughter of a very wealthy Beverly Hills Jewish family and her middle-class values were diametrically opposed to Frank's newly forming, more iconoclastic ones. In retrospect, according to Frank, partly as a way of dealing with his loss, he proposed marriage. In 1953, Frank, twenty-six and Joan, twenty-five, married at a lavish wedding in Beverly Hills. By the time of the wedding, Frank had already begun to have second thoughts about the marriage. During the long drive down to Acapulco on his honeymoon, Frank recounted, he did not utter a word to Joan, struck by a sense of having made a huge mistake. He realized he had committed to someone and to a way of life that were greatly at odds with how he saw himself and his life unfolding. During his years at the University of Michigan, Frank had begun to question main-stream, capitalistic assumptions. Even before that, he had made it clear to his father that he was not interested in taking over the family business or any other business for that matter.

He retreated into silence, his only solace from this catastrophic realization. Charlotte remembers how ill-suited they were from the beginning and attributes her brother's decision to marry as a reaction to the death of his father and to their unresolved estrangement.

After the honeymoon, Joan returned to Beverly Hills for a few weeks before joining Frank in Cambridge, Massachusetts. Frank returned to his Orchard St., Cambridge apartment to prepare it for her arrival. He began fixing it up in a style that reflected his Spartan values, reconstructing orange crates to serve as end tables and, thanks to the skills he had gained under his father's tutelage, installing his own effective, but perhaps unaesthetic, wire-exposed lighting system. When Joan arrived, she was appalled. Frank was stunned and hurt by her reaction. Without a job or much to do during the day, Joan found herself alone much of the time undoubtedly adding to a sense of homesickness. A grad student and also working, Frank was often not at home; and when he was, he would often retreat into his own work and thoughts. Joan had exchanged her parent's Beverly Hills palace for a monastery equipped with its own silent monk. Six months later, when her parents came to visit, they were aghast at the cloister-like existence their daughter's vows had led her into, and they insisted she come home with them. Frank and Joan divorced soon after that. Joan's family insisted that she keep all the gifts, including the diamond ring he had saved up to buy for her.

Joan's departure surely must have dealt another emotional blow to Frank who was still reeling from the loss of his father. On the other hand, it may also have freed him from the entanglements of a commitment to a life-style he was beginning to see more and more clearly as alien and repugnant to his developing leftist, pacifist values. After Joan left, in the fall of 1952, Frank asked a fellow journalism student, Don Friedman, to room with him in the very apartment that Joan and her family had found so wanting. Don and Frank had hit it off at BU. Don found Frank's unorthodox perspectives on the study of journalism intriguing.

According to Don, while most of the journalism students were grappling with practical issues for their theses, he remembers that Frank was writing his on something to do with "... esoteric Durkheimian theories on the sociology of journalism."

Although Don ended up moving out three months later because the neighborhood was too noisy, the two remained long-time friends, despite an early calamity that would have caused a rift in most friendships. Soon after Don moved in, Frank and another friend Noel, talked Don, who had never skied before, into skiing an expert trail at Cannon Mountain in Franconia, New Hampshire. This adventure ended disastrously, with Don breaking his leg. (Don would go on to become an expert skier, besting both of his beloved buddies and now lives in Franconia.) But Don had come to understand that in addition to holding unconventional intellectual views Frank was also a bit of a dare-devil. In the long run, he didn't let the skiing fiasco get in the way of their friendship.

When Don moved out in January, 1953, Frank also left the apartment and joined a cooperative housing arrangement not too far from MIT where his friend Noel Hicks, a math instructor at MIT, resided. There were about 6 young grad students, most of them at MIT, who were members of the co-op. Through Noel, Frank met other students and young instructors. A handful would remain friends throughout his life. The dearest was Bob Archer. Bob and his wife Nancy were members of the Friends Society who not only shared a strong commitment to pacifism and communal living with Frank but also, a love of the outdoors. Bob and Nan would introduce Frank to the American Friends Service Committee (AFSC) and the Appalachian Mountain Club. He frequently joined them on canoeing, hiking and camping trips. When Bob took a teaching position at the University of Massachusetts in Amherst, Frank would visit them there, and later, at their farm in nearby Leverett, spending time with their growing family.

The early fifties were a heady time for Frank. He had found a community of friends who were enthralled by the same provocative, philosophical ideas as he was. They rejected the excesses of materialism and committed themselves to altruism and pacifism. Frank's relationship with Noel was especially close. Noel was a handsome, charismatic young man from Wyoming, with a great spirit of adventure – physical as well as spiritual. He and Frank would take off on Kerouac-like, spur-of-the-moment trips to experience the rapture of being alive. Noel could bring out the exuberant, bon-vivant Frank, but he would also allow the quiet, introspective Frank the space he needed. Noel eventually took a teaching position at University of Michigan, Frank's alma mater. Despite the distance, their friendship continued to be an intense and deep one. Every now and then, Noel would show up on Frank's doorstep in Cambridge, and think nothing of asking him to drop everything and accompany him on some off-the-beaten-track quest.

I remember the first time I met Noel. It was just a couple of years after Frank and I married in 1970. He'd come to ask Frank to accompany him to Nova Scotia, to find a large, beautiful piece of driftwood he had stumbled across on an earlier trip there. Unlike Frank, Noel had a very calm and gentle manner, and yet they were kindred spirits. Their enthusiastic playfulness and passion for adventure was equaled by an interest in philosophy and abstract thought. I had witnessed Frank's exuberance before, one of the characteristics that was most attractive about him, but I had never seen it play off someone else as it did with Noel. Off they went the next day, as if they were still young grad students in their 20s, not separated by the responsibilities of wives, children and teaching careers. They returned successful, several days later, carting a huge piece of driftwood about 9 feet long and 3 feet wide shaped somewhat like an X. Frank named it the Lady because it looked (to him) like Venus de Milo. It came to adorn our back yard for years until it finally rotted beyond salvation.

The day they returned, I came home to find Noel, adept at yoga, standing on his head in my living room. We carried on a conversation in his upside-down state as if that was how discourse normally occurred. In 1980, when we returned from living in Germany for a year, Frank tried to get in touch with Noel. He hadn't heard from his friend in many months. Unsuccessful, he called Noel's ex-wife and was shocked to learn that Noel had died of cancer while we were away. She had had no address for Frank in Germany, and thus had been unable to get in touch with him. Frank was devastated by the news. Once again, someone he loved deeply had died while he was absent and unreachable. Generally an exuberant person, Frank's melancholy state lasted for months, which made it clear how important Noel had been to him.

In 1953, after finishing grad school, Frank decided to spend a year abroad. He joined a group that was being sent by the American Friends Service Committee (AFSC) to live and toil in work camps in Germany and France, building housing for the poor. He booked transport on a student ship, where he attended classes and studied French. Writing from the ship in July, 1953, he told his mother and sister he had "met a friend from Cambridge .... Who was also with the AFSC. As fellow pacifists we have led the force of non-violence on a ship full of quasi-militant nationalists. This has involved us in two and three hour long discussions in small group(s) which have proved to be extremely spirited."

Once in Europe, Frank headed for Germany. He lived and worked with many Germans whom he found kind and gracious. Even at this early stage of his life (he was twenty-five), Frank was developing a philosophy about people that militated against stereotyping and labeling. (This would later blossom into a strong commitment against labeling special needs children.) Here was a young Jew working in Germany less than 10 years after the world had uncovered the Nazi brutality and annihilation of the Jews, yet he was unwilling to categorically condemn the Germans. In August he wrote his mother:

...In your last letter you spoke of the "killer" that supposedly resides within some of the German or Russian nature .... It is easy to speak of some Germans being like this or some Russians (or some Americans for that matter), but is there really a "killer" nature that resides within certain national groups? Or is this what we are tempted to believe because of our own predisposition to justify our own actions? Let us not forget that the Germans were handed the same bill of goods to prepare them for war that we were and as the Russians are today. Thus they as we, were capable of things contrary to Hebrew, Christian, Democratic tradition. Just as we don't hear of the many injustices we perpetrated in the name of a just war, so the Germans were unaware of Dachau and Buchenwald. Since we were victorious the Dachaus and Buchenwalds were played up but the results of American and allied policy and soldiers has been wiped off everything but the minds of the Germans who lived through them. Individual Americans as well as individual Germans are capable of great cruelty.

After Germany, Frank went to France. He traveled over the Alps on a second-hand, single speed bike. Neither he nor the bike fared well on the trip, both collapsing after making it over some challenging Alpine heights. He was found and treated for exhaustion, by local residents. He was in France for a year. In Paris, he learned French, took courses at the Sorbonne, sat in on a class taught by Piaget, and worked a few days a month with the French equivalent of the AFSC, helping to rehabilitate housing for North Africans and other poor people. He soaked up the culture, language and politics. His weekly letters to Eva and Charlotte make clear that Frank was going through another heady transformation. In January 1954, after visiting a small Quaker community 150 miles south of Paris, he wrote:

> We worked, with pick & axe of course, clearing a road on a site which will be the homes of 100 French working families in a year or so. This is the work of a certain *Parisienne* priest who has attacked the problem of housing in a way that few people in France have – namely by building new houses. He has done this by organizing work camps consisting mostly of men over 40 who have two strikes against them- either because they have been to prison or because they are alcoholic etc. The priest, *Abbé* Pierre, gives these men a bed & board and directs them into groups to work on the housing projects. Thus he attacks the problems at the same time. It was an extremely small camp – only 15-16 *voluntaires* – 13 French. So French was just about the only language spoken. In terms of the spirit & the integrity of the camp, we reached an extremely high level… partly responsible for this was the way in which we lived – completely without comforts. We slept in a small unheated loft on some straw that we found in the neighborhood, and huddled together on the floor. A sleeping bag, several blankets, clothing, socks, sweaters kept one relatively warm during the night & one hardly heard the mice running around & playing. …It was a week of being cold and dirty- of hard work which one could not stop because of the cold- but all of this led to a group spirit… we would huddle around a fire after dinner. Usually one conversation sufficed of the whole group – when we tired of talking we sang – and the humor flew in all directions – well over

my head most of the time – French being what it
is and my knowledge of it being what it is!

After leaving France, Frank spent a few months visiting a
friend in Yugoslavia.

Even in his twenties, Frank had already developed a view,
influenced by anthropology and new theories in physics, that the
observer is an inextricable part of the observation; that observation
has to be subjective. This is illustrated in a letter written to Eva
and Charlotte from Yugoslavia about the conflicting values the
new communist states posed for leftist thinkers. It also shows
a certain humility in knowing that he just didn't have enough
information and insight to pass judgment.

> The conditions of a third class coach were
> my first Introduction to Slavic Europe. ...As you
> know, this is a police state... I am aware of the
> danger of reading into that which we observe...
> In fact I have done it and have been aware of
> the fact for quite a while that we MUST put
> ourselves into our observations. My position,
> from the start, has been an extreme sympathy
> [for] all those things that have been instituted
> in this country as an answer, as an attempted
> solution to the "primitive" state of affairs. On
> the other hand I have... strong if not obsessive
> antipathy against centralized patterns of power.
> For myself I would [not] sacrifice the latter for the
> former but ...I have seen here, that there are many
> millions of people who have made the choice ...
> in the opposite direction. Now I thrust myself
> into the situation and try to obtain some little bit
> of understanding...

In 1954 Frank wrote from Belgrade, asking the International
Voluntary Service for Peace to assign him to India for service.
His request was driven by a "desire to serve in a concerted and

constructive way for a better world." Service would contribute to the betterment of all, (including his own) and not just host country residents. Because of the extreme need in India but also because it was a culture that would require a great deal of understanding and change on his part as well, Frank felt that India was probably one of the best places to implement these views. He never got to India. While in Europe he was also applying for teaching positions in the United States, all in remote places. He was offered a teaching position at Patten Academy High School, in Patten, Maine. Patten is in Aroostook County, in the northern part of the state and, at the time, was one of the poorest and most isolated counties in the state.

It is unclear, though not surprising, why Frank sought relocation to a remote place. He had apparently developed a philosophy about 'service' that was as much about expanding his own worldview, as it was about giving. Perhaps he believed that it was at the geographical fringes, be they of the globe or the country, that he could best come to understand the fundamental essence of humanity. He started teaching history and social studies at the high school in Patten in 1954. By the time he made it up there, he had a dog, Calamus, whom he had found in a shelter and who had been abused. He and Calamus grew inseparable. Once, in the log cabin he had found to live in, in the outskirts of Patten, the wood burning stove caused a fire while Frank was asleep; only the efforts of Calamus woke him up and saved him. The family of a student in his class, Brenda Rogers (her uncle had rented him the cabin), took a liking to Frank and often invited him to dinner and to other family events. Their ways seemed easy and welcoming to Frank. In the spring, some of the Rogers clan took Frank white-water canoeing on the Penobscot. They showed him how to do it right. On one of those occasions they managed to split the canoe in two, the water was that fierce; this only made Frank all the more enthusiastic about white water canoeing.

Brenda's older sister Judy was in her last year at Patten Academy High that year. Frank and Judy started dating each other. Judy was the valedictorian of her class at Patten Academy and had been accepted into the Massachusetts General Hospital graduate nursing program. She would start the following September. By the end of the academic year they had decided to marry.

Frank's teaching career at Patten did not go smoothly. As would often happen in later teaching positions, he often deviated from the established curriculum. A strong believer in the philosophy of John Dewey, he took students out of the confines of the classroom and exposed them to direct experiences in their community. He was also never shy about challenging administration policy if he believed it was wrong. Exactly what Patten Academy rules he had failed to follow is unknown, however, in a letter from the superintendent, dated February 12 1955, Frank was advised, "At a meeting, last night, the Joint Committee of Patten Academy voted to give you 30-day notice of termination of contract … with the understanding, however, that should you continue to improve – in discipline and general deportment—as you have during the past week, the 30 days will then have been considered as a probation period, and you will be retained for the remainder of the school year. …". Frank was "deeply troubled" by the letter. He wrote the superintendent telling him that he was sure the "…present misunderstanding [could] be ironed out…" It wasn't, and on March 5, 1955 Frank received another letter from the superintendent: the Joint Committee had voted unanimously to ask for his resignation.

Judy had already left Patten for nursing school when Frank moved to Winchendon, MA, to a house on a lake, taking a teaching job at the high school in the neighboring town of Grafton. In the winter months, he'd ice skate over the lake to the school. Always a lover of sports, he was an avid hockey player and a graceful figure skater. Despite his agility, he managed to fall through the ice a number of times, including one time when he was on his way to school and his ice skates froze-up. He ended up taking the bus and teaching his class with his skates on.

Unfortunately, as at Patten, Frank had trouble with the administration of the Grafton schools, and was again fired. He held a number of teaching positions from which he was fired. On one occasion, he had his pupils subscribing to the *Daily Worker* as well as to some more conservative periodicals, so that they could begin to understand how much of what passed as objective reporting was no more than opinion. The parents complained to the administration and it became one of the reasons for his dismissal.

At the time Frank was teaching at Grafton, his sister Charlotte, her husband Don and their infant daughter were living in nearby Gardner. Charlotte remembers this as a difficult time for Frank. He would retreat into an impenetrable silence. "He was depressed, gloomy and hard to communicate with. Despite my efforts, I couldn't cheer him up, and neither could newborn Holly. He was trying to decide about the marriage to Judy and agonizing over it." His first marriage had been disastrous. Would he get it 'right' this time? He managed to resolve his fears and marry Judy on May 25, 1956. Right after they married, he took a job teaching eighth grade at Perkins School for The Blind in Watertown, MA.

Frank loved teaching at Perkins. He loved his students and fondly remembered the challenges they presented and those he presented them. Unlike his previous teaching positions, Perkins proved to be a very positive experience. Perkins would introduce him to the world of disabilities, a world for which he would become an ardent advocate for the rest of his life. He left Perkins on a positive note for graduate school.

Eva, Henry, Charlotte and Frank, Mt. Vernon, New Jersey, 1934

Frank in his early twenties

Don Friedman and Frank, skiing at Cannon Mt., NH, 1953

Frank, on left with checkered jacket, working for the Friends
Service Committee, France, 1955

FRANK AND JAY, TUESDAY, OCTOBER 27, 1992: "THE LACK OF INTEGRATION THAT EXISTS IN ME ALSO EXISTS IN THE INSTITUTION"

Frank: What occurred to me had to do with the role of braces in my getting to walk. The controversy is whether you just go with whatever a person can do. In facilities working with cerebral palsy, you go to some of them and you won't see a single person in a brace. They'll be teaching kids to walk and some of them will be on the floor crawling and other kids are being held. You'll go to another place and everyone is in a brace. There are braces for their feet and even for other parts of their body.

Now I haven't really gotten into this controversy too much. I was once exposed to vehement advocates of both positions and I can really feel that controversy in myself: whether you stick all the braces on and plod along, with the rationale that you're strengthening your muscles, you're being upright—which is important, just to be upright—as opposed to just getting help and support to walk on your own feet. Interestingly enough, I'm a real candidate for both approaches.

Now when Teresa comes back Wednesday, I will talk to her about what the alternatives might be. It's quite clear that this place is orientated toward braces; they have brace clinics. They'll make my own braces for me that will fit me. But it simply may not be necessary to teach me to catheterize or to make me braces. I may be totally off the mark on that.

Jay: Is Teresa someone who will be straight about that stuff?

Frank: I think so. I mean, she took me behind closed doors and used the Feldenkreis method.

Jay: To the layman, it would seem that developing your quadriceps, to have the knee strengthen through that kind of approach, would be better. But it's not just matter of strength, it's a matter of coordination around the knee, I suppose.

Frank: Ultimately it's a question of integration, as I've said many times, that your knees and feet and trunk and stomach work together, and for me they don't work together yet. What all this is about is getting them to work together.

Jay: What about a compromise in the form of elastic braces?

Frank: Well, they have some other ideas. One of the compromises was that one foot had a lock on it and the other one didn't, and that was a disaster. Either leave the braces off or put them on; lock the knees or don't lock the knees. The ironic part is, those braces are so heavy and so clumsy that it's very difficult to walk in them if you are, you know—

Jay: —in the best of shape.

Frank: In the best of shape. Arlene [physical therapist] said that she's going to put them on this weekend and try them out herself. I thought that sounded good. But, to my knowledge, she never did. They're very heavy, they're clumsy, and they don't quite fit right on your feet (laughs). And yet that's the task, to walk in those fucking things. Again, a good metaphor for much learning, much teaching, much therapy. We have other kinds of braces that we put on that are similarly clumsy. So, it's a dilemma for me, having an institution that clearly believes in braces.

Jay: Whatever their posture is about that, they should be willing to go over the pros and cons of each approach or to put you in touch with someone who could.

Frank: Well, I agree that that would be nice but this is not that kind of institution. This is a military institution in several respects; there are chiefs and there are workers. The chiefs make the decisions and the workers carry them out. Furthermore, there isn't very much communication among staff about a lot of things. The lack of integration that exists in me also exists in the institution. Besides, the assumption of the institution is that when I'm ready to walk, I'll walk.

Jay: I hear your thirst to know something about what each approach has to offer; you need to have that information if for no other reason than to feel that, whatever approach is used, you can put yourself into it. It would be very nice if the physical therapist and the occupational therapist could sit down with the MD who is saying you have about eight weeks to go, and map out a plan to get you there.

Frank: Well, I'm sure that the occupational therapist and the physical therapist don't know anything about that.

Jay: Is that a place where the psychiatrist could be helpful?

Frank: He ain't going to help me very much. He's outside of the hierarchy and really he wants to be outside of the hierarchy even though he was intrigued with my discussion with the director.

Jay: Well, he's low man on the medical totem pole. What would happen if you were to raise this with the director?

Frank: I might.

Jay: By the way, was Aura able to read my hieroglyphics? [notes for Frank's letter to the director]

Frank: Yeah. She picked them up and looked them over and that seemed to have everything in it. She took them home and I don't know if she's going to have a chance to work on it tonight. She said that her life is so jammed up between work and Anelisa, Dylan and me.

Jay: Again, I come back to what resource could the School of Education be. Just as they sent a chair car for you for that party. From a pragmatic point of view, the quicker you are on your way to recovery, the more is in it for them.

Frank: I don't disagree with anything you said, but the logistics of getting things done…a lot of people asking you what they can do, and you try to tell them, and eventually someone will come through. (laughs) That's the way I look at the University.

Jay: So you're dubious that if the dean knew of your needs he would be in a position to do very much about it.

Frank: Well, I'm not so sure that I could tell him exactly what my needs are. Explaining about the controversy, and the need to know more about it, and so on. I spend a whole semester talking to students like that and I don't get through to half or three quarters of them. You know, really they don't understand the nature of these applied fields and the total inability of any one approach to dominate other approaches in any kind of therapy, in any kind of teaching—whether it's behaviorism or psychoanalytic approaches or psychodynamic approaches.

Nothing ever dominates; and to get students to really understand that and to read about it and to get a feel for it and to see how it impacts on themselves or on other professionals is a major challenge. That's what we're saying about this issue with braces. There's a very deep controversy in the field. I don't know that much about it, but I've had some contacts with it and I feel it very personally in terms of their using the braces on me. I know there is something there, but I think it would take a pretty sophisticated person to sort it out.

Frank and Jay, Friday, October 30, 1992:
"The fucking struggle goes on and on"

Frank: Well just to chronicle an eventful day. It started in the middle of the night at one o'clock or so and this woman came into my room, this nurse's assistant. I tried to talk to her ...I didn't get a smile out of her; I didn't get anything out of her and I was extremely uncomfortable and I needed a urinal.

Jay: Was this a new person you have not seen before?

Frank: Never seen her before; she kind of put the urinal on me and when I asked her to move me, she said she couldn't move me alone, and she walked out. I was in misery for a long time. Finally she came back and removed the urinal and said I was all wet. The way she put the urinal in was sloppy; it didn't permit me to adjust it like it is now. So then someone else came in and took care of me fine.

Then this woman came in again with someone else. I couldn't communicate how I wanted to be repositioned. The two of them tried to get me in a certain position, and they couldn't get me there. Finally they just walked out of the room, and there was no nurse's button; you couldn't even call up anyone. I couldn't do anything and I really became frustrated, lunging and lunging until I was able to pull the nurses' wire out. You do that and it just blinks on and off.

Eventually someone came and I said I wanted to speak to the head nurse. And eventually she came … (Frank dozes off, resumes) Yeah, the head nurse came in and the woman was there and I said, "She didn't do the job, you know, she wouldn't straighten me out, she claimed she couldn't do it alone, and she misplaced the urinal." Just a whole load of things she had done wrong. Meanwhile, I was burning and aching on my butt, as a result of this, and I am to this very moment. I made it a big issue during the day. I told the patient representative, and I told the doctor, how incompetent and almost cruel this nurse was. After that was resolved, I got another nurse. (dozes off) So that was one series of events that really marked my day. Hurt my back and made the therapy difficult, made it difficult for me to sit up or anything.

Later on in the day, I had some exercise with someone in the physical therapy room. When she got me back to the chair, she dropped me—which is difficult to do, since I really carry my own weight; but she wasn't experienced. It was a real crisis. I was hysterical. I was mostly on the floor, and she didn't know what to do, and there was no one in the room. We yelled and finally got the attention of — (dozes off)

Jay: Who came when you yelled?

Frank: I yelled and screamed and finally someone who is an office person came. The student therapist who had dropped me told her to go find a therapist some place. Finally, there were five or six therapists around who started problem solving and got a sheet and a stretcher. They picked me up and put me on the stretcher and then on the couch. By that time, I was trying to make light of the thing. One of them, later on, said that I had dealt with it graciously. I was laughing and making jokes; I said I had never seen the bottom of the table or the physical therapy mat from that position. I had never seen their faces that way. I made a lot of jokes about it and got over my fear when I realized there was nothing broken. There easily could have been a broken leg or something. It was a *horrible* experience.

The third thing that happened was that we had a team meeting. Aura couldn't be there, so I met with the psychiatrist and members of the team; only the doctor wasn't there again.

Jay: Did the team include the physical therapist and occupational therapist?

Frank: Yeah, and the head of nursing. And the primary nurse.

Jay: And the purpose of the meeting was what?

Frank: To discuss my treatment plan. I mentioned that I was very positive about what they had done, and that most of my complaints were not about the people in that room. The head nurse said things weren't as rosy as I had made them seem and that there was a lot of frustration.

Jay: A lot of frustration on whose part?

Frank: On the part of the team.

Jay: With each other? With you?

Frank: With me, because I was resisting their eating plan at lunch. Their plan was to have me eat alone. That became the big issue. I realized then that it was a mistake to have this meeting without Aura, because there were five or six of them. I don't think they all agreed, but no one was going to speak out against the head nurse. It's just too hierarchical a place.

Jay: Hierarchy and discussion don't go together.

Frank: They claimed I could eat alone. I claimed, "What's the big deal about giving me someone for 15 or 20 minutes. I'll eat alone to the extent that I can." They didn't listen. Finally I said, "Okay, try it for a week. The net result will probably be I'll get cold food and I won't eat very much."

Then they said they want me to change my breakfast plan, too. Instead of eating after going to the bathroom and getting a shower and getting fixed up and brushing my teeth, they wanted me to eat at seven o'clock or seven thirty. I said I didn't want to eat then. They insisted that's part of the rehab plan. We went round and round; finally I said, "Are we negotiating something or are you just telling me what you're going to do?" The psychiatrist intervened there. Eventually they agreed they would just do the lunch time eating plan and the other we would hold off on, talk about it again. This whole discussion was about the eating plan, whereas the head nurse claimed it was about my rehabilitation.

Not much was accomplished, except that I agreed to go along with them for a week; I don't think there was much of an exchange of information. Certainly, there wasn't much of an exchange of compassion. At this psychiatrist's urging, they agreed to drop the breakfast plan for the time being, although clearly, that's what they have in mind. They claimed that it would give me good training, good experience. It seems to me a more a question of control.

Jay: Now when you say 'they', who is joining the head nurse in saying this, anybody?

Frank: The OT, the head nurse and Nancy, a primary care nurse. ... So that was the day, these three rather excruciating experiences. Just fighting and fighting and fighting. Fighting night nurses; fighting at team meeting; and being dropped and having to get up, having a burning hot rock on my bottom, which I have right now as I sit here.

Jay: It sounds like just a *shitty* day. It's like the dropping of you is symbolic of what went on in the conference. They dropped you. They're not paying attention to you. Not that it's pleasant, but I think you did absolutely the right thing to fight. You've got no alternative but to fight this. I think you're right, there should be an advocate, Aura or someone with you, when you meet with them. These are *tough* negotiations. I would be happy to be there if I can. **(they discuss the time of the next team meeting)** Well, it sounds like if you can make it through today, you can make it through any day.

Frank: (chuckles) But also today, I walked in an incredible way. More control, more—

Jay: —with braces or without?

Frank: With braces. But I was doing everything I wanted to do. My whole—that thing you read to me about the difference between intent and action—was minimized. I intended to walk and I did walk. My sister was there counting steps, and we figured I walked well over a hundred steps.

Jay: Really!

Frank: Almost every one of them was something I wanted to do and could do and did do. So, that also happened today. Plus they did a lot of work on my left arm; I don't know that it meant very much.

Jay: Your progress continued, whether it was a lousy day or a good day.

Frank: I don't know. Problem is (cries) I wonder what battle will be tonight. Eight more weeks of these fucking battles!

Jay: Hopefully, this night nurse is a one shot deal. One of the things your fighting does is get her out of the picture.

Frank: Well, I made it clear she's not for the hospital. But I do get this idea (in tears) that there will be a struggle tomorrow with one of them. It's almost as if it is programmed. That is what is so horrible about it. Why couldn't they fucking well say, "Okay if you want to eat in your room, eat in your room". What difference does it make?" Give me someone for fifteen minutes.

Jay: Frank, it seems to me as if faculty and students, if they knew, could make a point of being here at lunch time.

Frank: I don't want that! There's so many people who are here so much of the time, and that is a tremendous burden on Aura. It has gone far enough. Now she arranges for mornings, hiring this woman, Cindy; and [other friends] coming in and her coming in. It's gotten out of control. It shouldn't be so at a hospital like this. That you have to make all these fucking arrangements without necessarily having to get special care, but without having to worry about being alone. Being alone, when you are on your stomach like I am, and no one's here. I slip down. Aura said to me, "Well, I'll come at noon." Well, I don't want that, that is no answer to anything.

Jay: No, I agree with you about that.

Frank: I mean, why be in the hospital if you are going (laughs) to make arrangements for people to be here 24 hours a day!

Jay: Sure, but on the other hand, I think there are a lot of people who, if they knew that that would make a difference—it's not a pain for them, they would be delighted to do that.

Frank: Maybe so. But it's eight more weeks, I don't want to. I feel it's already too much of a commitment by too many people.

Jay: I think people care about you, Frank.

Frank: (in tears) They do but, how much can you ask? There is a limit—and not only that, but you shouldn't have to ask. You got to, somehow, get to the core of this fucking place and change it so the fight doesn't go on all the time! The fucking struggle goes on and on!

I think it's a real deep problem of their program and how they run it. How they want to control people with—

Jay: —you of all people, accusing you of being dependent! They are just not tuning into who you are!

Frank: That's what I told them. I told the psychiatrist, I *never* don't get up for a therapy session. I always push for more. If they want ten leg raises I give them fifteen. ... But the real issue is the institution and its control of people within it and its inability to really take seriously my control. My dictating whether or not I have breakfast in a certain way. I did finally say, "I'm not going to eat in the hall." They apparently accepted that.

Jay: They may still be smarting from that.

Frank: Yeah.

Jay: Were they the ones that initiated this meeting today, or you?

Frank: The psychiatrist. And he told me privately, and then in front of them, that maybe the problem is that I intimidate them because I am a professor, and I am bright and articulate. Now, how that fits into this picture is beyond me.

Jay: Well, they are used to running the show... it's like nurse Ratchet [in *One Flew Over the Cuckoo's Nest*], she didn't want someone taking the ball away from her. It may be that is what's really going on. And they are going to go after you until there is an advocate there who says "look!". You can say it but you are in a certain role.

Frank: I think so. I think that when *I* say it and it sounds like I'm just resisting.

Jay: Sure, they will interpret it like an analyst interprets a patient's—

Frank and Jay (together)— resistance.

Frank: So you lose either way.

Jay: Well, in a screwy kind of way I think today's meeting is good from a diagnostic, strategic point of view. It makes clear what the enemy's position is. It's a shame to have to look at it that way, but it feels like an adversarial relationship.

Frank: Yeah, they deny that. The psychiatrist said, "It's not you against them; we are all out to help you." And that is dangerous stuff. Maybe the psychiatrist is not the friendly witness we thought he was; maybe he is, underneath it all, a hostile witness.

Jay: He's part of the system, no matter how much of a renegade he may be. It's like what some Quakers accused other Friends of believing, "We're here on earth to help other people but what on earth, other people are here for, I don't know!" (laughter) So, there is some of that in the mix. Yeah, I'm almost certain I can be here for that meeting on Wednesday. -- So, are you through with the urinal?

Frank: I did a lot; but I may have a little more, though.

Jay: In a weird kind of way, Frank, you have a chip you hold against them with the falling. There was a real appreciation, on some people's part, of the way you handled that because you really could have stuck it to them. You could have a lawyer in and scare the living shit out of them!

Frank: But they have a chip on me too. I can't walk out of this place and walk into another place.

Jay: Sure, but, you are still a God damned *customer*! You paid all these years for the insurance that is paying them!

Part IV. HOME AT LAST

Although in constant pain and unable to walk alone, Frank is ready to go home. He speaks of the hallucinations brought on by pain medication. He confides his concern for Aura's health and his belief that, despite the demands of his care and her outside work, she needs the independence and stimulation her job offers her. Tired of his inevitable conflict with the staff's many unwritten rules for being a good patient, he decides, with Aura in agreement, to leave the hospital.

Once home, he looks back on the valuable parts of his hospital experience – the space to explore and its variety of people. With Aura and Jay he talks of the return to home life.

HOME AT LAST - JAY

Back home,
released
from institution's grasp
Frank faced
his lot
with hope

but he had learned
that fortune's tides congeal
in paralysis' winter world:
with spinal injury
things go in circles

Frank braced
for recovery's
riled waters,
bolstered by
family
and a view
of worlds
he might ply

he couldn't see
the tidal wave:

Jay Clark and Aura Sanchez Garfunkel

night terror
neural chaos
relentless torment
bearing down upon
his coracle of hope;
random mercy
blocked his view

how could
he have lived
had the furies
announced
their aim
before they struck

amidst hope's shards
he endured
each night's travail,
counted minutes
to distance pain,
pursued
blind alleys
of medication,
physical therapy,
massage

day by day
Frank lived,
hour by hour
found
respite moments,
sudden joy
hid within
attrition

years later,
medication
sprung his world
from pain's grip
at last,
allowing
wild adventure
and conquests
long deferred

FRANK AND JAY, TUESDAYS: NOVEMBER 3, 10 AND 17 1992: "IF I BROKE THE RULES I WAS GOING TO GET PRETTY BAD TREATMENT"

Toward the end of October Frank began to anticipate leaving the hospital. Increasingly, he realized that the hospital was outliving its usefulness. While his walking improved, pain arrested his progress and nights became more terrifying because of the lack of response to his calls for assistance.

The following three conversations are presented together as they are concerned with the issue of Frank's leaving the hospital

Jay: You recorded Saturday and this is Tuesday. I know you had a rough Sunday morning. But then you said you had an excellent PT that day. You did a lot of walking, as much as you've done.

Frank: Yeah, good walking. A lot of ability for me to do what I wanted to do. That is the key to it, whether my body obeys my mind. Today, it didn't work that well, and I think it has to do with the fact that I have a lot of pain. Maybe because stuff is returning and my body doesn't know how to deal with it.

Jay: Pain in other areas besides your butt?

Frank: No, my butt mostly. The main pain is in my butt and in my arm. And it doesn't let up, no matter what happens. It prevents me from doing and thinking about other things. Lately, Aura and I have been talking about how long I can stay here—how long I can stand the place, even though a lot of it is very pleasant. The evenings and the early mornings, and now, some of the early evenings, are pretty ugly.

Jay: The early evenings?

Frank: Well, the nights are bad, because I don't sleep that well. Sometimes they have floaters or other staff that are difficult to explain to—what they should do to assist me and why they do it.

Jay: By the way Hy [a friend] had some thoughts about pain management.

Frank: I'd like to talk to him about that. The little I have done of it has tended to work to a limited extent, I don't want to take medication, I really don't.

Jay: Basically, what he says is to try to control the pain not just by reducing it, but by increasing it; seeing what you can do to increase it with your mind and then bring it down and see what that does.

Frank: We had a student a few years ago who was into that.

Jay: Well, I'll give Hy a call and talk to him about some of that.

(Frank falls asleep)

* * *

Frank: Lately, sleep deprivation has been so bad that in the middle of the morning I'll be riding in the chair and I'll fall asleep! (laughs) Fall asleep at the wheel, and very, very difficult to deal with it.

Jay: You seem to be more alert tonight, like you got a good night sleep last night or you had a nap or something. Is that so?

Frank: No. I think I had my phase of falling asleep earlier in the day—and I'm not having it now. I've been taking some medication to alleviate stiffness and pain, and when I do wake up,

I hallucinate; I think I'm someplace else. This morning, I told the nurse I needed to get up so I could go to the bathroom. She said, "You can't go to the bathroom," and I didn't know what she was talking about. I said, "Come on, I can't get the sheets out from under me, they are preventing me. Just help me get the sheets out so I can go to the bathroom." She again said, "You can't go to the bathroom." She never really explained, "You know, you have a spinal injury." She didn't lead me out of the hallucination; she just denied it. I thought that was interesting—that the nurse, who I like a lot and is very caring and everything, had no technique to deal with my tremendously anxiety-producing dilemma.

Jay: Well, not only no technique, but no awareness. It seems to me that there is a certain level in human relationships that children go through; they begin to realize that someone else has a totally different experience, a totally different perception. It takes a certain degree of sophistication.

I was talking with a special education director this morning about that. He gets in trouble with parents of children with special needs because his staff won't accept the fact that a parent has a different point of view. They just feel defensive about their own, and they tell parents, "You are wrong", just as your nurse did. It seems to me that one of the key forms for training teachers or nurses or anyone who is interacting with people is to realize and respect that whatever the person is saying is their own point of view. Whether it's objectively right or wrong doesn't matter.

Frank: The first night I took this pain medication, it apparently had no effect and it was a horrible night. I would ring the bell and no one would come to change my position. I watched the minutes roll by, and it seemed like truly an eternity of time and of exhaustion and pain.

The next night, I woke up and thought I was in Mount Auburn hospital [in Cambridge]. There is no question I was seriously agitated. And that nurse—who I also like and is also very caring—simply said, "No, that is not where you are and you are in your regular hospital." She did things like saying, "What's your name; when is your birthday; where do you live?" So I established that I knew all these things and she just left me. I was overflowing with anxiety; it was very, very scary. It was three hours before I was able to calm down about it.

At one point, she said, "I know this is a very disturbing thing to you and if you want me to, I'll call your wife." So she had an inkling. I thought about it and I was going to have Aura called, and she would have been over. I probably should have done that; but I couldn't see—I mean, Aura is really under strain. I don't know if you looked at her tonight—between the job and Anelisa and me and her allergies—I don't know if you noticed, but her neck was all scratched up.

Jay: No, I didn't notice.

Frank: It's a childhood thing she used to do; her neck would itch and she would scratch and scratch.

Jay: It's too bad there isn't someone over there at work who recognizes what she is going through and says, 'Look Aura, just take off. Look I don't care, just get out of here, we'll handle it; we'll tell people.'

Frank: Oh no, they have given her that liberty.

Jay: Yeah, but—

Frank: —and I don't agree with you. If anything, she needs to work and I need to make sure she works. And she is working part time; she doesn't have to go in any day she doesn't want to. They put absolutely no pressure on her, so I think they are doing the right thing.

It's like when Aura went to law school. We both believed that if she didn't develop her own métier, her own life, our marriage was going to fall apart. I was intensely involved in what I was doing and she was taking care of kids and doing some volunteer work that didn't satisfy her. She really needed to do what she eventually did: go to law school, become a lawyer, get a job and make some money, and begin to develop her independent life. This is another example of that: she needs to have that life out there in Chelsea and do the things she does and go to the meetings she goes to.

Jay: I guess what I feel is that part of her tension is how to fit it all in.

Frank: Well, one way to fit it in is to get out of this hospital. I think for quite a while the hospital was a positive factor with negative things to it. Now it has become a negative factor with positive things to it. The negative stuff is overwhelming her and overwhelming me. We make these remarks about how come they don't have something for me to answer a telephone. Or the nurse walks out and forgets to shut out the light, and so there I am with the light open; I can't shut out the light. So much dependency is built into the system here.

In the beginning it was a pain in the neck; I've now found out something about the treatment process, you know, the obvious stuff. But you and I are discovering other things about it: the people, the relationships, the perception of change, the fact that it isn't so bad if patients have to be vigilant in order to get what they want.

Jay: You know, you are getting as close as any patient will get to the system as a whole, with your letter to the director and your meeting with the director of nursing and the meetings with the physicians. And yet, for all that contact, you are still basically in the same dilemma.

Frank: I noticed one time, I was really in bad shape and I didn't ring the bell. I got tired of ringing the bell. And a nurse suddenly appeared; she said, "How are you doing?" I was shocked by it. She did about two or three minutes of shifting me around and walked out, and I was suddenly comfortable for a little while, maybe only a half an hour. A little later, I didn't ring a bell and she stopped in again.

I realized that is what has to go on. Whenever you get help because you ring the bell or turn the nurse's light on—that's one kind of help. Another kind of help is when someone comes in and says, "Can I help you? Do you need a new position?"

Jay: Non-crisis intervention.

Frank: Well, it is crisis intervention.

Jay: But there's a different quality to it; it's not like you precipitate the crisis. Someone checks in with you and gets information.

Frank: And you don't ask for the help, you just get it. So if I had that kind of attention, it doesn't mean having my private nurse. This might be very naive and unrealistic—is it possible to have people who check in on people, given the supposedly short staff they have?

Jay: I fear they budget down to a bare minimum.

Frank: I had another conversation with one of my physical therapists. I said, "You know, this beautiful area with these great mats and parallel bars is used five days a week about six hours a day; thirty hours a week. And they sit there the rest of the time unused. Why shouldn't patients be able to use them at other times? I was in one of those areas and I was kicked out because there wasn't a therapist there. Why couldn't a patient come in and get on the mat or be transported to the mat and do some turnovers or even just lie on the mat and go to sleep and use the place?" She said, "Well, you couldn't do that unless there was someone here." So I said, "Okay, so there is one person here and six or seven people using the mats.

Jay: Like a gym.

Frank: She thought about it and she said, "That would be a good idea. But on the other hand, most of the people don't have your motivation." So I said, "Which comes first, motivation or having the space available and encouraging people to use it?" She said she would recommend it, but that she didn't think it had much chance of getting through.

Jay: It would be ideal for you to be at home at night and come in during the day, spend four or five hours here and do PT and OT. Even if the gym were being used, they wouldn't be using all of it all at once. You might be able to be in there while people were using other parts of it.

Frank: It all depends on whether we get an extension of our hundred days of in-patient insurance benefits and we don't have an answer to that yet. If we get an extension, we can do it here or we can do the home hospital care service. If we don't get an extension, then on December thirteenth we're on our own.

Jay: I can't believe they would just cut you off!

Frank: Are you kidding! There was some woman in for braces today. The brace guy said, "You bring the check. You don't bring a certified check, you don't get the braces. That's it". This kid who was my roommate, they said to him when he was ready to go home, "If you don't have the Medicaid card number, you don't get anything from us, we can't even put you in the ambulance." So it's a real business, a severe business.

* * *

Frank: I think what I discovered in the last 3- 4 days is that I tended to view all people as being either good or bad. Now I think it is this: there are a few people around who I am convinced will do almost anything for me, no matter what the situation is, or what time it is. Then there is another bunch who will do quite a bit, but it has to be the right time or the right thing. And then there are quite a few where you really have to ask them in a certain way, at a certain time.

I realized that before this, when I was in agony I'd wait and wait until a certain amount of time had elapsed. Then I would call, and if it was enough time, then they would come. I thought about my being able to figure out what their rules were. If I could figure them out, I could get by. If I broke the rules I was going to get pretty bad treatment. The more I thought about that, the more discouraged I became about this place. I was systematically putting myself through torture so I could obey their rules. I was just going crazy, waiting for the clock to go around, so that enough time would have elapsed so I could call on them to switch my position.

That seemed to be a breaking point for me. I realized I can't take it anymore. If they say, "What should we do at night to make you happy so that you can sleep?" I would have to tell them to break the rules. It is not administration rules, it is really staff rules.

Staff rules are built around certain realities, but I have become very cynical about those realities. For a long time I thought they were too busy, not enough staff. I don't believe that any more. I've been talking to a lot of the other patients and they all tell the same horror story, about putting their hand on the button, waiting an hour and being ignored. If that's true, if everyone is telling the same story, they [staff members] are taking their time off: they are not around, not available.

Jay: It is very hard for administration to know about that. Your attempt could have prompted a quiet or not so quiet investigation. It would be a marvelous thing if, at some point, you could come back here, not as a patient but as an observer, a researcher, and just be around. I doubt that that's ever happened. Ex-patents and ex-students have visited their institutions, but not quite in the way you might conduct it if it were to happen.

A week after this conversation, after nearly three months of hospitalization, Frank returned home in the family car, driven by Aura. A ramp from the street to his front porch had just been completed so that he could be transferred by wheelchair from the car to his bedroom in the former dining-room.

Although disapproving of Frank's discharge, the rehab hospital did recommend a care facility, Wellmark, that provided hospital-level home care. This included home health aide, a nurse and a therapist, coming every day; and a doctor and a social worker visiting once a week. Later, with financial help of Mass Health, the state insurance for handicapped people, Frank and Aura were able to hire a Personal Care Attendant.

Jay Clark and Aura Sanchez Garfunkel

During the first months at home Jay and another friend, Al Murphy each spent one night a week with Frank. Other nights were covered by Aura or by attendants from Wellmark.

EXTRANEOUS - JAY

Frank spoke
of trials,
conflicts,
triumphs;
I listened,
queried,
encouraged him
to tell
his tale

at times,
I rhapsodized
in my own key,
radiating advice,
selections from
my book of wisdom

sometimes
when I paused
Frank changed the subject
or napped
oblivious to
his visitor's
treasure

my wave
absorbed
in sand's
indifference

as I recall
our talks
I blush
at my persistence
to light his way
with my lamp

in thrust
towards remedy
I see
my wish
to straighten
his necessarily
crooked path

FRANK AND JAY, FRANK'S HOME IN WINTHROP, MA, TUESDAY, NOVEMBER 24, AND FRIDAY, DECEMBER 4, 1992: "A DIFFERENT KIND OF GETTING BETTER"

The following two morning conversations are presented together because they are brief.

Jay: So we have been talking about the transition—

Frank: —how different the space is, how different the people are, how different the routines are—

Jay: —and how, to some extent, you've been suffering from deinstitutionalization, even though you are happy as hell to be out of there.

Frank: Yeah, I slept four or five straight nights, six or seven hours each night. Getting up many times, but Aura would just turn me over or do something to my feet.

In a way, it has been very painful, because my legs do get frozen up or they get all cramped up, but I go right back to sleep. We usually sleep with the house at 55 or 60; it took us four nights to realize that I can't take 60 degrees, even with all those blankets on.

Jay: Maybe you're slowly acclimating: you start at 70 and work it down. Sort of a parallel to the whole transition; your entire system is undergoing the shock of what seems like a fairly easy and comfortable change.

Frank: I had such painful experiences at the hospital at night—and during the day too—where you called for people to help you and they wouldn't come. In the house, there is always some one with me; here is always someone who is going to respond. And yet, I don't know... it's not that I miss the hospital, well maybe I do miss the hospital, or certain things about the hospital.

Jay: You had nine floors plus the outdoors, and that had to make some difference.

Frank: Here I have the two or three rooms that I can wander around in, and a bathroom that is being built, and a lot of clutter. Half the time, I can't even get into those rooms. I've got to acclimate myself to a very, very different environment.

Jay: Plus there was a cast of characters that kept filtering in and out, a whole range of characters. This is a more intense environment, in a way. The people here are important people, but the environment is more contained. You really don't have a daily routine quite established yet, I assume, or do you?

Frank: No, I got home Friday. There is no program on Saturday and Sunday. Wellmark has people coming in, but it is a much more limited array of people, although I think they are as high if not higher quality than at the hospital, and much more committed to the idea of patients receiving therapy and beginning to adjust in their communities, their homes, their own beds, their own environments—

Jay: —but you're a person who enjoys the stimulation of all those people coming in and out. I think of the night we had Chinese food at the hospital and there were seven or eight of us sitting around. Not that that can't happen here, but there was something about the impromptu nature of that place; suddenly people would show up and things would happen.

It is going to be a couple of weeks before the rhythm of being here hits its stride and the bathroom is ready. I think there is a lot to be discovered, just as you discovered a lot of things about the hospital in the first couple of weeks you were there and wandered around.

Frank: And then this other issue that we talked about: as you rehabilitate, you have the expectation that you're going to feel better, that you're going to sleep better, that you are going to show signs of getting better. I guess with a spinal injury it doesn't work that way. You go up and down, you go around in circles, you go on a roller coaster. There is this long term expectation that the big word is *return*: things are going to return. But in order to get that return, you've got to go through a lot of pain, your ass is going to hurt and your legs are going to hurt and get heavy, and it is a different kind of rehabilitation, a different kind of getting better.

* * *

Jay: This is breakfast time on Friday, after a six and one half hour sleep, of course one of the more successful nights. [Jay's first overnight with Frank, at home in Winthrop]

Frank: Now we have got to be concerned about the progression of successful and unsuccessful nights. The night before, when Al was here, was a nightmare: a lot of thrashing around in the bed, a lot of pain, a lot of aggravation even when I finally did go to sleep.

Jay: And you really slept very quietly last night, I mean the first part you were on your back, snoring, you hardly moved at all. I was wondering whether you would feel pain in your bottom when you woke up, but you really didn't. You were stiff, but you didn't have any significant pain, I guess—

Frank: —whether it is a result of medication or it is a result of just the ups and downs of—what do they call it again—

Jay: Neuro firings?

Frank: Neuro firing muscles or—

Jay: —exercise may make a difference. You did a lot of exercising before you went to bed and Gwen [nurse] recommended that I massage your feet before you went to bed, (weird tape noise)

Aide: [from kitchen]: Oh, this is what we smelled, Oh Lord! (recorder has been placed too close to the wood stove and the cord is burning)

Jay continued his overnight stays with Frank but their conversations went unrecorded while the tape recorder was being repaired.

A LIFE UNBOUND: THE LATER YEARS (1957-1998) - AURA

Frank often spoke with fond memories of his tenure at Perkins School for the Blind. The fact that the students were blind or vision-impaired never stopped him from teaching in the same unorthodox ways he had taught before. He sought field trip opportunities to get his students out of the classroom, interacting directly with their environments. He pushed his students to try things no one would ever dream of having blind kids try.

A few years after Frank's death, I received a call from John Beaulieu, one of Frank's students at Perkins. As a thirteen-year-old in Frank's social studies class, he had taken the role of Eisenhower in a play the students wrote, based on the upcoming 1956 election. Frank encouraged John to write his own lines in his portrayal of Ike. John took to the task eagerly and did such a good job that Frank suggested he send a copy to Eisenhower in the form of a letter. John typed it in Braille and Frank translated the words over the raised Braille lettering. Eisenhower was apparently quite impressed and replied to John. Many years later, in 2003, when the National Archives decided to set up an exhibit on Eisenhower, John was informed that the two letters would be displayed. John immediately called Frank, excited to share the news. Over the years, John had maintained sporadic contact with Frank. Alas, his excitement turned to disappointment and sadness when I told him that Frank had died five years earlier. He couldn't believe that it had been five years. If only he'd seen him before he died. They had always talked about getting together. He and I spoke on the phone for a long time. It was comforting for me to hear John's stories about Frank; his believing in his blind students' potential and treating them as one would, students with sight. "We made a Panama Canal and a map of South America. Frank asked me to teach for half a day. He made me feel like a human being; the best teacher they ever had at Perkins. Frank had built me up. Before Frank I was a drifter. Frank boosted my morale. But after he left I was adrift again." Several months after talking with John on the phone, my daughter and I had the opportunity to meet him and his wife in person. We invited them to come see (and hear) a film my daughter had produced, in tribute to her father. We were surprised they actually came and were delighted to meet them.

Despite his fulfilling experiences at Perkins, Frank was also eager to get back into academic studies. After Perkins, Frank and Judy moved to Indiana, where Frank accepted a position at Purdue University. Their son Max was born there. They lived in Indiana from 1957 to 1959. Then they moved to the outskirts of Storrs, Connecticut, where Frank took a position as an assistant professor in special education at the University of Connecticut. They rented one side of a big farm house in Storrs; the other side was rented by the yet-to-be-famous singer Judy Collins, and her husband and child. Frank, Judy and Max lived there for three years.

Things were not going well in the marriage and when Max was four, Frank and Judy separated. The separation was not something Frank had wanted; he found it excruciating when the time came to leave Max. Years later, he and I went to see the movie "One Potato, Two," the story of a racially mixed couple who has a child and then they separate. The woman, African-American, is forced to give up her child to the father, who is white. Frank talked about how difficult it was for him to watch the movie; how much it brought back the anguish and pain he felt when he was forced to leave Max; how he had sobbed. Judy and Frank divorced in 1964. Frank moved back to Boston, enrolled in a doctoral program at Boston University in special education, and soon had a teaching position in the same Special Education Department. Eventually, Judy left Connecticut and moved around the corner from Frank in Cambridge, allowing Frank and Max to live close to each other once again.

The chairman of the Department of Special Education at Boston University was the charismatic Dr. Burton Blatt, a zealous advocate and prodigious writer on behalf of the rights of retarded individuals. Frank and Burt hit it off. They developed a deep respect and love for each other. Burt was amiable and funny. He understood and came to rely on Frank's brilliant and creative thinking about issues in the field. He also understood that Frank's often sharp and iconoclastic approaches would never get him congeniality awards and sought to insulate Frank from faculty hostilities. He provided Frank with a shield and in turn, Frank provided him with the kinds of provocative challenges Burt needed and thrived on.

In the mid-sixties, Frank received a special grant from the Department of Education to evaluate the integration of handicapped children into Head Start programs. A number of programs throughout the United States and Puerto Rico had been chosen randomly for evaluation and Frank's team was assigned to Mound Bayou, Mississippi, a black community. Soon, the parents and the white B.U. evaluators were frequenting lunch places together that had been nominally integrated. Restaurant staff would put up screens to keep them out of sight from other white patrons. It was apparent that this would inevitably result in trouble, and yet none of the team felt they should avoid going to lunch with the brave black parents of Mound Bayou.

Unsurprisingly, one afternoon, Frank was arrested after one of these lunches, on trumped-up charges of drunken driving. One of his colleagues, Sandy Alexanian, immediately called Senator Kennedy's staff, who intervened to ensure that Frank was at least placed in an isolated cell while awaiting arraignment, away from any local prisoners who might take 'justice' into their own hands. After a few days he was out on bail and was advised to plead <u>nolo contendere</u>. Whether it was the United States Marine Corps, the State of Mississippi, or eventually, the autocratic rule of President John Silber of Boston University, Frank was not about to kowtow to rules he thought were unjust. After that, his Mississippi stint came to an end, although he did keep up correspondence with a few of the activist parents of Mound Bayou. He never forgot the parents of Mound Bayou and came to the realization that one of the most important values of Head Start was the role it gave the parents. Head Start was both a pedagogical tool and a political tool for community organizing and change.

Although an academic, Frank was also very much an activist, passionate about securing legal rights and social equality for disabled children. He saw these as advances on the road to social and political inclusion for all marginalized peoples. To him, it was ultimately about equal protection under the law. He advocated for the passage of landmark legislation at the state and federal level that would mandate free and appropriate inclusion of special needs children in the public school classrooms of America.

Frank was adamant about the issue of 'labeling,' which he railed against because it over-simplified and reduced individuals to two-dimensional entities and failed to take into account individual manifestations of a disability. One size could not fit all. He also believed that personality was dynamic, influenced by relationships that in turn influenced achievement. A child could excel or fail depending on his/her relationship with his/her teacher, or, for that matter, any other adult responsible for fostering learning and growth. He believed people existed, as within a prism, each part of a person being a composite of the relationships the person had with others. In other words, the relationship of a disabled child with the teacher was critical.

In the fall of 1968, recently separated from my first husband, I moved to Boston from Washington, D.C. with my five-month old son Dylan. I was temporarily living with friends, Alex and Barbara Rodriguez. From them I heard somewhat legendary tales about Frank Garfunkel. Alex had first met Frank at a controversial and heated community meeting in Roxbury, where some of the black leaders in the community were questioning the federal Head Start requirement to begin accommodating special needs children. A panel had been convened by Reggie Eaves, a prominent black leader in the community. Both Frank and Alex, who was then director of the Cooper Community Center in Roxbury, had been invited to sit on the panel. Frank spoke about the moral necessity to include handicapped children in Head Start programs.

Frank's assertion engendered heated disagreement among a number of people who were running community programs for poor black children. Failure to abide by the new requirements would endanger any federal funds a community agency was receiving at the time, so it was an issue they couldn't easily walk away from. Some became hostile, yelling at Frank. They were already serving poor black kids, they said, who had many strikes against them; it was outrageous for the federal government to require them to expand programs further to include blind, deaf, and severely disabled children who would require burdensome and expensive accommodations. Frank grew increasingly impatient with reactions he assumed were disingenuous. He accused his opponents of being hypocrites, arguing that such inclusion was no different from racial inclusion – the same fears, concerns, and fundamental rights were at play. Alex was stunned by Frank's refusal to back down in the face of what was becoming a major confrontation, and was impressed by his logic, feistiness and passion. After the meeting, he invited Frank to go for a beer. It was the beginning of a long and close friendship.

Soon after I moved back to Boston, Barbara Rodriguez planned a dinner party so that I could meet some of their new friends, including Frank. Another couple brought along a neurologist friend, Giuseppe, who was visiting them from Italy. They thought that perhaps Giuseppe and I might hit it off. I was amused at how polar-opposite the two available male guests were from each other. Frank was boisterous and irreverent, Giuseppe, suave and serious. I found neither one of them especially appealing. Giuseppe was a bit boring; Frank was too strident.

A few weeks later, Frank happened to come over again. By now I had heard from Barbara about Frank's intellect, iconoclasm and *joie-de-vivre,* but that evening I was struck by his reserve. Alex and Barbara's friends included community organizers, ex-Goddard College students, hippies, recent Harvard Law grads, Puerto Rican and black community leaders and like-minded South Enders – a true hodge-podge. They laughed, played the guitar, sang, danced, got high and discussed the burning issues of the day. Towards the end of the evening, a heated political debate ensued. Frank sat back quietly listening, as strong opinions were voiced. After a while he spoke, just a few words, but what he said surprised me as real and compelling. I realized that I might have judged him too hastily. A few weeks later, at another gathering of friends, Frank and I met again. This time he was in a wonderful mood; very light and very funny.

We began to spend time together: going skiing, to the movies and taking trips to visit his friends. He was indeed complex and before I knew it, I had fallen deeply in love with him. He challenged my thinking, but at the same time saw wonderful things about me that I had not known to exist. Friends of his would tell me that he was a changed man – that he seemed gentler and they attributed this to me; that I had softened him. I had no way of gauging. All I knew was that he was so supportive; he made me feel that I could accomplish anything I wanted to. I had never felt that way before. Frank was warm and demonstrative, easy to love and easy to be loved by. Whatever I did was always met with praise (no matter how poorly I did it) and this would continue until his death. After about a year of seeing Frank, Dylan and I moved in with him to his Granite St. apartment in Cambridge. Although we had our share of disagreements and arguments, made more difficult after his injury, throughout the twenty-seven years we were together, we never lost our love or respect for one another.

Frank and I married on July 7, 1970. Several months later, he took a sabbatical leave and we traveled to Europe, ending up in Israel. We had bought a VW camper van in Amsterdam with the intention that we would travel through Europe, take a ferry from Greece to Israel and then cross over to Africa, to Tanzania. We were both fascinated with Africa and since we had a year, thought this would be the most interesting way to travel. Israel was on the itinerary because Frank wanted to visit cousins of Eva who had migrated there from Poland. Unfortunately at that time, a cholera epidemic had broken out in a number of places in the middle-east and we were told that crossing borders would be very difficult. We were also informed that getting into Egypt would be problematic with passports stamped with an Israeli visa. In addition, I had become pretty run-down in the month or so that we had been traveling through southern Europe.

Accordingly we decided to travel directly from Europe to Israel via Greece. After a fairly turbulent ferry ride from Athens to Haifa, we immediately drove to Kfar Yehoshua, where Frank's cousins Chaim and Chana, their son Yoram, and his wife Nira lived. They were so warm and welcoming that after being there a couple of weeks, we found it hard to leave. Through a friend who had met Frank at BU we were able to find and rent a spacious house in Nayot, a new area of Jerusalem and Frank got an appointment at Hebrew University as a visiting professor. We had Dylan, who was two and a half, and Max, who was eleven, with us. I stayed at home with the kids, studied Hebrew, and took sculpture lessons at the Israel Museum. Israel was fascinating, physically, culturally, and spiritually. We found the Old City of Jerusalem intriguing. I would take long walks through the narrow streets and alleys, admiring the array of foods and goods sold in the open air stalls and the mixture of religious cultures that converged on the ancient streets. We took camping trips with Frank's cousins, to the Golan Heights. We drove along the almost empty roads of the West Bank, stopping in such historic cities as Bethlehem, and were shocked and dismayed by the Palestinian refugee camps. We went swimming and snorkeling in the Red Sea; camped in the Negev; climbed Masada; and spent Chanukah, Purim, Passover and other holy days with Frank's family.

It was idyllic but also a rocky year for us. We were newly wed and each had brought a child to the marriage. We had no support system to turn to in moments of friction or crisis, and there were many, including a miscarriage. Max, in particular, was unhappy. He missed his mom and resented having to share his dad with a new wife and a two-year old. Somehow we made it through the year.

On our return to the states we bought a turn-of-the-century house on Winthrop Bay in Winthrop, Massachusetts. Frank bought an old wooden boat, a Lightning # 44, which he spent many hours coating with fiberglass because of its bad leaks. Despite the drudgery of prep work, he spent many exhilarating hours sailing his almost leak-proof Lightning on Boston Harbor. The early 70's were especially fruitful years for us. Seth was born in 1971 and Anelisa in 1974. Frank's department was thriving, on the cutting edge of academic thinking in Special Education. He had about a dozen doctoral students preparing to make a difference in the lives of disabled children. Towards the end of the decade however, things began to change. Burt Blatt left BU to take a position at Syracuse University. With sadness, Frank assumed the chairmanship of the Special Education Department. John Silber became the new President of the university and quickly managed to alienate most of the faculty and student body. As a result, the faculty unionized.

As a faculty member in the forefront of the struggle with Silber, Frank agreed to become the first president of the new union. Constant confrontations with the administration on the one hand, and with faculty on the other, took a toll on him. Not only did he have to deal with a hostile administration, but with dissenting views among the faculty as to how they wanted to proceed vis-à-vis the administration and what they wanted from a labor contract. The issue of whether to strike was the most contested. Despite the anguish and toil expended by the warring faculty, their union was decertified in federal court. Faculty members were to be considered managers under the National Labor Relations Act and therefore could not unionize. Silber's strong, authoritarian governance would prevail.

In 1976, I enrolled at Northeastern Law School in Boston. During my second year, Frank was offered a position in the BU overseas teaching program in Germany; BU had a contract with the armed forces to offer graduate level courses. When he first told me about the offer to teach abroad, he was sure I wouldn't go along with it; after all, I was in the thick of law school. He was surprised when I jumped at the Idea. I knew it would mean postponing graduation, but I also saw it as a rare opportunity to expose the kids to another culture. Fortunately, I succeeded in getting a six-month internship with the Judge Advocates General (JAG) Corps in Heidelberg that allowed me to fulfill half of the law school's cooperative work requirements. Indeed, it did turn out to be a most significant year for the five of us.

The kids fell in love with living abroad. We did a lot of camping, touring and sightseeing. Dylan and Seth attended the US Armed Forces School on base and Anelisa went to the local kindergarten. (By this time, Max was 19 and studying at Boston University.) Ever the advocate, Frank was appalled by the Department of Defense, (DOD) Schools' disregard of Public Law 94-142, the Education of All Handicapped Children Act. Frank challenged DOD on their lack of compliance with this law, which required that all schools receiving federal funds provide a free and appropriate education for all disabled children, in the least restrictive environment. DOD was not even trying to comply; they argued that they were exempt from the law. When Frank's concerns appeared in the U.S. Army's newspaper, Stars and Stripes, the administrators at BU admonished Frank for his outspoken criticism of DOD. Academic freedom notwithstanding, they made it clear that Frank would never get another overseas teaching appointment. Their threats did not intimidate Frank and he continued his criticism of DOD for its failure to comply.

We returned to the states in August of 1979, enriched and deeply affected by our experiences that year. We vowed to do more traveling with the children whenever we could. We engaged in a number of home exchanges over the ensuing summers, mostly in Europe. In addition, during the years when the kids were in public school, we would spend February school vacation skiing in New England, and April school vacation visiting my mother in Hormigueros, Puerto Rico. Travel had become an important and integral part of our family life-style. It was an interest Frank and I had each brought to our marriage that was eagerly absorbed by the children, not only for the sense of adventure, but for the excitement of learning about new places.

During the early eighties, Frank's beloved mother, Eva, began to develop Alzheimer's disease. Frank had a great aversion to institutions, stemming in part from the work he'd done on institutions for mentally retarded children. He had strong beliefs that once a person was institutionalized, it was the beginning of the end. Eva came to live with our family in Winthrop, but after two years, her behavior became potentially dangerous to herself and to the rest of us. We knew she could not remain at our house, even with the care of a personal attendant. There were times when she'd leave a burner on; other times our neighbors would find her outside crossing the street with only a slip on, with her cane and her handbag. With the last remnants of her self-censoring mechanism lost, the more objectionable aspects of her personality were accentuated. If she didn't like what you were saying, she wouldn't hesitate to pick the cane up in a menacing sort of way, although thankfully she never managed to land it on anyone's head. There were times when she did things that in a tragic-comical way made us laugh. We had two sets of little stairs, one from the kitchen, the other from the foyer, leading up to the longer flight that went to the second floor. Eva would start up one set thinking she was going up only to come right back down the second. And she would do this several times before we'd realize that she was literally 'going around in circles'. One of us would then accompany her upstairs. I became more and more frustrated by Eva's condition – her inability to finish sentences and thoughts, her wanderings off, her stubbornness. We tried to make her act reasonably and speak rationally, and in so doing we became the irrational ones; we knew she couldn't and yet we behaved as if she could.

For me the culminating event was when Anelisa then about eight, called to say she was going to a friend's house after skating which usually let out around 5 PM. Her friend's mother would drive her home, sometime around 8 o'clock. She left the message with Eva who was to make sure she'd let me or Frank know. Of course, Eva did not tell us. We were frantic. It was not like Anelisa to come home late without calling. We were ready to call the police. When she finally arrived, I burst into tears at the sight of her, hugging her at the same time I was asking where she had been. Surprised by our degree of alarm, Anelisa became frightened and began crying saying over and over again, "But I called and told Nana to tell you I was going to be late." I began to feel as if I too was unraveling. Although it was difficult for Frank to see his feisty, independent mother deteriorate, we both realized our home was no longer a safe place for her to live.

Eva went into a nursing home in Concord, NH, near Charlotte's home. She died, in September of 1990.

After finishing law school, I went to work for Greater Boston Legal Services as a poverty law attorney. While at times our life was punctuated with the excitement of summer and school-break vacations or winter ski trips, it was the in-between, day-to-day events of our familial life that most fill my memories. On cold winter mornings, Frank would be the first one up, going down to the kitchen to make a fire in the wood-burning stove. He'd also put the coffee on and make cereal for breakfast before rousing the rest of us. We'd huddle around the fire with our coffee or hot cocoa and look out across the cold blue waters of Winthrop Bay. Our home is right on the water, facing west toward Logan Airport and the picturesque cityscape of Boston. Every evening thousands of office lights and their reflections in the blue-black waters of the bay twinkle back at us. When they're accompanied by dazzling sunsets, the spectacular colors and shapes can be intoxicating. In subfreezing temperatures, glacier-like slabs of ice form on the beach, helter-skelter on top of each other, caused by the moving tides, creating a moon-like surface.

After the kids had scurried off to school, we would go to work, Frank dropping me off in Boston and oftentimes picking me up after work as well. We had an intricate web of after-school surrogate parents, the most popular being my father who would live with us for about half the school year. We all adored Papi, as he was called by everyone. Papi was the grandparent who really got to know the kids: their quirks, their loves, their fears, their talents, and their individual uniqueness. They loved being with him, and, in turn, they had a transforming effect on him. He became a special person for them that no one else got to share. Frank would look forward to Papi's arrival and the calmness and joy he brought to the household. When it was time for him to go stay with my sister in New York, or with my cousin in Puerto Rico, we'd all become sad, not wanting him to leave.

Although none of us was religious, we always celebrated Christmas and Passover, cherished holdovers from our respective religious upbringings. We also loved to have family gatherings and parties – big parties with lots of friends, food, dancing and singing.

In the summer, when we weren't traveling, our family doings took a slower, more vacation-like existence. On hot and humid days, we'd just go out to the end of our dock and dive into the cold waters of the Atlantic. Frank would usually teach one of two summer sessions at BU, which meant he had the rest of the summer off to tinker with our Boston Whaler (that had replaced the old Lightning), perform household chores neglected during the winter, or take the kids out fishing or water skiing. There were times when Frank and the kids would pick me up in the whaler after work, docking at the New England Aquarium. As soon as I'd see their relaxed, sun-tanned faces, all the stresses and worries of representing families who lacked what mine was so lucky to possess would melt away, and I'd happily surrender myself to the slapping waves of Boston Harbor. The Harbor was an important presence in our summer lives. The kids would go to camp for two weeks out of the summer, but after that, the Harbor became camp. We'd explore the Boston Harbor Islands, go camping for a couple days on our favorite, Great Brewster Island, or just go out fishing for the evening meal.

Most of the conflicts Frank and I had with each other were mundane, usually having to do with the kids, often triggered by different child-rearing philosophies or perhaps more accurately by our different personalities. Frank thought I was too indulging of the kids; I thought he was too demanding. Looking back, I now see these as healthy differences that in the long run benefited Seth, Dylan and Anelisa. Today, as young adults, they look back on their interactions with their parents and laugh at some of our absurdities. Dylan remembers Frank as having an obsessive love affair with wood. If he spotted a piece of driftwood in the harbor, everyone was recruited to go out and lasso the piece to the boat, dragging it home. The piece generally lay in the yard until it could be used for something – sometimes it could be for years.

As for me, one of the many jokes, was the ridiculous pains I took to advise the kids about cars: safety belts, not driving fast, not drinking and driving - all the usual no-nos. They would joke about it, telling me that it had been their every intention to drive crazily – that is, until I told them not to.

The situation with Max was substantially different, however. From the beginning, Max deeply resented Frank's new family. He strongly contended that he had been shut out after our marriage, even more so after Seth and Anelisa came along. We each held different versions of events he would often recount as evidence for his contentions. Over the years, there were numerous heated interchanges and letters between Max and Frank. Max's anger caused Frank hurt, frustration and sorrow. Max insisted on delving into the wrongs that he felt had been committed against him, while Frank, a strong believer in not dwelling on the past, would often say to Max that there was no point in belaboring the past. They each looked at the past through such different lenses. Frank felt it would be more constructive if they could talk about how to move forward in narrowing the gulf that had grown between them. But there was never any resolution or reconciliation. Whatever the truth or truths were, Frank and Max, ironically like Frank and Henry his father, never reached rapprochement.

On August 27, 1992, while playing his beloved game of squash, Frank suffered a contusion of the spine that left him quadriplegic. The ensuing years were rife with pain, expectation, disappointment, fear, anger, and nostalgia for what had once been; there was a sense, at every level, of having to go back to 'go' and start all over again. At the same time, they were full of the realization of how important each one of us was to the other. For six years, Frank struggled, not only to overcome his pain and loss of independence; not only to re-learn to use the remnants of muscles that had once been robust; but to recapture the self he had been before the injury. There were months, years even, when his state of being was torturous – when he was extremely depressed, despondent, even suicidal. Things began to change with his ability to control the agonizing pains that tormented him all the time.

Yet, despite being trapped in the tentacles of quadriplegia, Frank never stopped challenging, questioning, wondering, loving, laughing. At the same time, because of this entrapment, he became a wiser human being: this new, formidable experience, like so many others in his life, was the cause of this metamorphosis. "To think I thought I knew what I was talking about," he once said to me when discussing his professional field of disability. At another time, he marveled at how he had all this time now to talk and listen to the kids; time that before had always been so rushed with other mundane activities. His injury afforded him the time to enjoy his children.

Frank with Max as a baby, 1961

Aura and Frank, Mt. Vernon, NY, 1977

Frank sailing in Boston Harbor, mid 1980s

Aura, Anelisa, Eva, Frank, Dylan and Seth in Winthrop backyard, 1976

WHEN DUSK DESCENDS - AURA

Relentless quills pierce
with voodoo menace –
deflating our spirits
casting our hopes up against rocks
hidden by an inundating tide.
Like appalled disciples
damning their guru for having sinned,
we curse a life

once secure as cotton
candy on its cone,
swaddled
in soft eider down.

Splashes of salty freedom
only memories now: boating
to the harbor islands
riding converging crests
of churning waves
like cowboys at a rodeo.

Camping in New England forests
where fragrances of pine
swirled 'round aromas

of skillet grilled bacon
and brewed Andean coffee.

Holidays, once in high relief
are sepia images of a past.
A panoply of pains consumes us.
And yet, when dusk descends
and we sit for supper
we still make plans
to greet the sacred daybreak
of tomorrow.

FRANK, JAY AND AURA, FRIDAY EVENING DECEMBER 18, 1992 AT FRANK'S HOME: "IT'S A VERY FINE LINE BETWEEN BEING INSENSITIVE AND BEING TOUGH"

Frank: Look at our new bathroom. Isn't that something?

Jay: Yeah!

Frank: They are going to start tiling tomorrow. They're determined to get it done by Christmas.

I continually claim that I can't sleep, and that's horrible—to go every night and not be able to sleep. I suddenly became aware today that I do sleep an awful lot during the day. If you had asked me that two days ago I would have said no.

Jay: Little cat naps here and there?

Frank: Yeah, but I realize that I *really* sleep during the day, and it is just impossible for me to sleep at night; so today I went on a real crusade to limit sleep during the day. I had Dylan wake me up after a half hour of sleep. Then Aura and I had some coffee, which I hardly ever have, and so I don't know how successful I have been; it is very difficult to reverse this cycle and start sleeping during the night rather than during the day. But my principal observation was how long it took me to become aware of this and to internalize it.

Jay: Well, the medication makes it hard to always be aware of your state of consciousness, I would think. If it gets to the point that they can cut down on the medication, you'll feel more alert. If they can fix this computer, you can spend part of your day reading or doing stuff with it. Are you spending any time reading during the day?

Frank: Not very much. During the day I am tired, because I haven't slept the whole night, when I try and read, my eyes are closing and opening.

Jay: What about the physical therapist and occupational therapist? Are you doing the walking or stuff that tires you out?

Frank: Yeah, I'm doing exhausting stuff with them; they are very aggressive, much more aggressive than the staff at the hospital. They keep on telling me, "You think we are aggressive now, we are going to really get aggressive." Some of it annoys me: they want me to put my shirt on by myself and brush my teeth by myself, and I don't see any relevance to it. Some of it makes a lot of sense—actually using the muscles to get out of bed. They see my being able to get up by myself, and sit up, and then get into the wheelchair by myself.

Jay: Really!

Frank: Yeah, that's what they are working for. Meanwhile, the exercises they give are exhausting, and sometimes I can't even do them because my legs just won't work. This program has very specific goals and there is less of the 'one, two, three go' and more of 'are you ready, stand up.' So the program is seriously different with these people. It's focused on walking, rather than building up general strength. Why don't I lie down, for a while, just grab my feet.

Jay: All right, let's make sure not to knock this recorder over. Do I make the first move or do you? (**Jay helps Frank get into bed and adjusts his pillows and blankets.**)

Frank: The other assessment they have made is that I'm not distinguishing between pain and something else. The doctor has quizzed me quite intensively as to what I mean, because I've claimed I have had intensive pain, and have taken so much anti-pain medication. The pain medication leaves me all stiff and I don't like to take it.

Jay: So your goal is to get down to no medication eventually.

Frank: Or to get down to a very common, generalized medication.

Jay: Well, that seems to make sense, because that has to affect your sleepiness in the day, along with your not sleeping at night.

Frank: With this new awareness, I see that the pain is a function of not sleeping [at night] and sleeping during the day. In that sense, it is ridiculous to take the medication. It is kind of irrelevant. The nurse is telling me, "Look you have got to not sleep during the day," and I say, "I would love to not sleep during the day but how do you do it?"

Jay: Well it sounds like they're basically willing to fight with you in your own behalf. That feels sort of right to me; it is going to lead to an intense dialogue. You're going to be able to persuade them about some things and they are going to persuade you about some things.

Frank: Well, at least I suddenly developed an awareness that I just didn't have before.

Jay: So in the last few days, have they changed the medication in any way?

Frank: Most of the decision about medication has been done with Aura, not me. I just am so medicated I can't discuss the medication.

Jay: I've noticed that you're moving your legs and your body around more, and I wonder if that helps ease the pain in some way.

Frank: Well, I do have new socks on with treads on the bottom, do you see those treads? They make it much easier to move around; now I can go like this. (pushes on his sheets with his feet)

Jay: I would think that all that motion just has to help that area in your buttocks to loosen up the muscles, even though it's painful.

Frank: They feel that I'm contributing to the problem by not sleeping well. They don't want to blame the victim, but they're almost blaming the victim—at times, they are. They said, "We're worried about Aura. We feel that if she doesn't get sleep, this whole thing is going to break down." And I said, " I'm worried about Aura, too. Those two things go hand in hand." I thought it was insensitive of them to make the distinction between their worry about Aura and their worry about me. They consented to provide 11pm to 7am staff to protect Aura, not to protect me.

Jay: Well, it's an interesting way to look at it. What it reminds me of, Frank, is the battle that Helen Keller's teachers had with her. A good teacher is ready to battle with the student, as a good student is ready to battle with the teacher. It's a very fine line between being insensitive and being tough, really challenging somebody, as you do your students. What I hear in your description is your respect for them. You may not always agree with them, but you feel they're solid people who know what they're up to. Is that fair to say?

Frank: Yeah. To a certain point I'm concerned that, one day, they might say, "Well, we can't deal with you. You sleep all day and you've got all of these odd kind of feelings. You're just a difficult—they've said many times to me. "You're an unusual case."

Jay: What do they mean?

Frank: That I'm not responding to the therapy and getting better in a consistent way.

Jay: Really? Some of them have been impressed with how much progress you have made.

Frank: Yeah, just the other day the nurse said "You know, Frank, your progress is consistent and we're all excited about it." And on the other hand they say, "You're an unusual case."

Jay: Well, you are an unusual case. Quite apart from the physical aspects of it, you're someone who wants to know. You're someone who is going to challenge anybody who works with you. You're someone vigorously invested in getting better.

(Frank needs to be adjusted and Jay works with him to make him more comfortable)

Jay: Good.

Frank: They wouldn't feel it was good. They wouldn't think I was working hard enough. They wouldn't think I was using my elbow and my wrist.

Jay: Well, they're not here! Are your muscles incapable of doing the eating and dressing or have your muscles not done them for so long that they don't know what to do? If the latter sense, pushing you is helping the muscles relearn what to do.

Frank: At Wellmark they would think that the role of the therapist is to teach you how to use those muscles. The basic role at the hospital was to just keep you in shape, so that when those muscles come into play you'll be ready to use them. Very different.

Jay: This sounds like a much more appropriate way of going at it.

Frank: Much more aggressive. "You've got to relearn this stuff; it's going to be quite a struggle." When I get up they want me to *get up,* to use my wrist and elbow. They want me to struggle by myself—

Aura: (entering, having finished cleaning up in the kitchen) Did Frank tell you he fell this morning?

Jay: No.

Aura: He doesn't tell you those things! (laughter) He fell. It was a kind of gentle fall. He was trying to exercise his abdominal muscles, so he says.

Jay: (to Frank) Were you on the edge of the bed? Where were you?

Aura: The commode. He plays games on the commode.

Frank: I was on the commode. I went over and I kept on going over and I went right to the floor (laughs) —

Aura: —and then we heard, "HELP, HELP, AURA, AURA!" (laughter) And the next thing I knew, he was on the floor. I got really scared.

Jay: Well, it shows he can fall on the floor and live to tell the tale. He's indestructible!

Aura: Then, he kept insisting we call the fire department. Rose [home health aide] was here, and Seth and Dylan helped; the four of us lifted him up and put him back in the bed. Fire department! (laughter)

Frank: I took a lot of abuse. (laughter) What did you accuse me of doing? Horsing around?

Aura: Playing games. He sits on the commode and gets bored. (laughter)

NIGHT JOURNEY - JAY

From darkness
comes a whisper,
Oh boy! Oh boy
I hesitate
do you dream
or lie awake?

we left port together
at evening
the ceremony marked
by brushed teeth,
in full regalia—
your sweat suit
at attention,
bed rails up,
thermostat set
to glide between
the fiends
of cold and heat,
meds stowed
to still
frayed nerves
on night's passage

Jay Clark and Aura Sanchez Garfunkel

your calls
arrested
our voyage
take the blankets off
move my legs
can you adjust the elbow patch
I need something to eat
alterations
to alter
the unalterable

slowly
through the night
expectation's fabric dissolved:

yours, to evade torment
mine, to ease your journey

pain drew you inward
to private refuge
and I, alone
gathered intention's shreds,

no bound to set
no place
to say 'no more,
not now'

no matter what I offer
put the blankets on
take them off
your thermostat commandeered
by severed nerves

I dance with your restlessness
your needs
surmount
my charity,
your demands
outstrip
my will

trickle of air
through window
threads to outside world
red digits in dark
mark distance
to shores
of endless sea

no act of mine
will make
things better

I become
like you,
a solitary sailor

your voice
penetrates
my reverie,

Jay, I need help
I stagger to my feet
protest
cast aside,

Jay Clark and Aura Sanchez Garfunkel

your cry
resounds
in me

and we
are back
together

Frank, Jay and Aura, Monday, December 21, 1992: "And he said, 'My name is Frank Garfunkel and oh, I'm on ships'"

During the first few years after the accident, Frank's pain loomed over everything else, even his utter dependency. We went through numerous medications—anti-inflamatories, ante-depressants, narcotics. Most would end up causing him to become groggy or hallucinatory. - Aura

Jay: The shortest day of the year.

Aura: (having lost track of time) Oh my God!

Jay: We're now moving back, as of quarter of ten this morning, toward the sun.

Frank: And every day from now on is going to be longer.

Jay: That's right.

Aura: (to Jay) Well, two nights ago, Frank got up and he said, "I have to do this by myself." And I said, "Do you want me to help scoot you up?"—by that I meant that I would hold his feet, while he would push himself up toward the head of the bed. But he said, "Oh no, I have to do this all by myself because Mrs. Green wants me to do it by myself." I said, "Well, who is Mrs. Green? Is it your physical therapist?" and he said, "No, It's her mother."

He kept referring to Mrs. Green, and consequently he did scoot himself up without me—(to Frank) because you were so adamant about Mrs. Green wanting you to do this by yourself. So at one point I said, "Frank, there's no one but you and me! There is no Mrs. Green!"

"No, no, Mrs. Green wants me to do that by myself. Isn't that right, Mrs. Green? Mrs. Green, Mrs. Green!" (laughter) I was laughing hysterically. This Mrs. Green had quite a hold over Frank.

Then he took his left arm, which he usually babies and doesn't allow to go anywhere, and started pushing it, trying to grab the railing on the left, because this was going to help him scoot up even more. Just the idea that he was allowing it to fly out there was impressive.

That was two nights ago. Last night, he got up in the middle of the night and said, "Would you mind pushing it over? Would you move my foot, do you think you could move my foot?" I thought I detected a slight difference in his voice. And he proceeded to talk in what sounded like a British accent. He wanted to know who I was, and I told him I was his wife. He said "Darling, do we have any children?" I said "Yeah", we had four, and told him the ages. And Frank told me that he was surprised at their ages—

Frank: —that they were so old.

Aura: I said, "Who are you? Where are you from? What do you do?" And he said, "My name is Frank Garfunkel and oh, I'm on ships." He had a friend. "And the friend and I work on ships." He was very nice, very polite. (Jay laughs) He said, "Oh, look. There's a Christmas tree over there." (all in accent) At one point, I thought he was going to break out in ancient Hebrew and prove that people had prior lives. (laughter) But he stuck to English.

Jay: That fulfills Jung's notion of the shadow personality. (laughs)

Aura: So he was very nice, very cordial. We had this conversation. And when I finally sat him up by the side of the bed, he said to me, "Did I forget everything?" I said, "You didn't forget anything, you're just hallucinating." Then he said, "How long will it take me to remember again?" But Frank says he remembers clearly both nights and the conversations, which is interesting.

Jay: Well, I think basically we're a collection of personalities. People who are abused may have had those personalities fragment, so that they're detached from each other. Most of us learn how to use a primary personality, but all the other personalities are there. If the right circumstances come up, we use them, I think.

Aura: Yeah, well, last night was definitely a personality thing.

Frank: It was also a repetition of this theme of strangeness, of being someone else, in some other place. I often get up in the night and I don't think it's my house, or my room. Just like I didn't think the hospital was in Boston. I often look at the room and I'm disoriented as to where it is; I'm in England or something.

Jay: Who knows. Possibly, you had an ancestor that lived in England and there's some genetic memory passed along. It doesn't come from nowhere.

Aura: What's interesting about that is that you [Frank] rarely imitate accents. I've never heard you do that.

Frank: One time, I was claiming that someone had been killed, and I said, "look in the bed and see who else is there."

Aura: "It's very funny," you said, "because they wanted to take my body and use my body instead".

Frank: Right, I thought that someone had been killed and they were using my body.

Aura: I could feel the bones going crazy.

Jay: It may be some kind of integrative process, some instinctive search on your body for memory traces that activate or move certain muscles. That would be very hard to document. There's a quality in that of breaking out of your mind set and doing something differently.

Aura: Yeah.

Jay: It may be that your hallucinations are very powerful dream fragments that require you to move differently or to integrate differently. It's during a period when you're doing a lot of new things, and their impact may get into your system.

Aura: It's almost like a perfected visualization. The rational, conscious, cautious part of you that's activated during the day is not there. There's no other part of Frank that's saying, "Be careful, don't get near me, my arm is sensitive, be careful with it."

Jay: Fascinating.

Frank: Complicated. I'm getting a lot of cramps. In my calf.

Aura: (to Jay) Just massage it. My brother-in-law [a psychiatrist], said that we should leave the radio going and the light on and that would help Frank orient himself a little better when he's up in the middle of the night. He came to the conclusion that they should put him on Prozac. Apparently the doctor, independently, had come to that conclusion, so he's now on Prozac.

Jay: And that is replacing?

Aura: It's replacing Tegratol and they're going to drop the Atavan unless he needs it for anxiety or for sedation. The Prozac has a stimulating effect as a byproduct, but it's primarily for pain and it's an antidepressant. It has the value of not being a sedative—if anything, just the opposite—and of interfering with non-acute pain. In addition, he's going to take, twice a day, this MS Contin which is a morphine-type drug, which is also going to deal with the pain. It's almost like a timed-release kind of thing so he won't have the rushes and then the subsiding—are you falling asleep? Frank?

Frank: Well, the pain in my leg. It really is bad.

Jay: It's in your calf as a cramp?

Aura: How about the heat? Do you want me to put the heating pad on?

Frank: Yeah, I think we need to do that.

Jay: Maybe the muscles are reacting to the fact that they're getting a workout. Are you moving your hands differently?

Frank: They're very annoying, my hands are. I often get in certain positions and I can't control them. They suggest that you flatten the hand out, [to counteract the cramping] bend it back and hold it.

Aura: My brother-in-law had some interesting insights into the pain; he uses drug therapy a lot. He helped to explain this whole business of Frank feeling his feet freezing, and the burning coals, and all that. What happens when those nerves are regenerating is that they start giving the message to the brain of heat or cold, even though there is no heat that's causing that signal. It's all these nerves doing their job, absent the stimulation. He was saying that there are newer antidepressants, such as Prozac, which interfere effectively with those pain sensations.

The pain is also very psychological. It's based on past as well as future experience, and a lot of it is really subjective.

Jay: (as conversation turns to an accident his son, David, had while driving on a snowy day in Portland, OR where he is taking a year off from college to earn money for travel) So he's getting an education by being out of school.

Frank: Just like my family. They're getting an education by my being so helpless. How do you shut the wood stove flue? Things that I've worked out over twenty years, and it's impossible to tell them how to do it. I tried to tell Aura how to adjust the flue this morning and finally Dylan worked it out, I guess.

Aura: You just have to hurry up and get better.

Frank: So you can remain helpless! (discussion of completing bathroom for Frank's use; he'll be able to shower in a few days, something he enjoyed at the hospital and is looking forward to. Frank hasn't been out because it's been so windy.)

Frank: You know, we went out on the trip, Saturday and it wasn't that difficult to transfer me into the car. So we have to do that more regularly.

Jay: How is it to ride in the car?

Frank: It was nice being in the car. It was a little scary the way this guy [friend] was driving.

Jay: Did the aide go along with you?

Aura: The aide didn't show up, which was just as well.

Frank: But I think we're going to go out for dinner Saturday night, because it's Seth's birthday, Sunday.

Aura: Yeah, he's going to be twenty-one.

Jay: Wow!

AURA'S PERSPECTIVE:
RETURN TO HIS CASTLE

By November Frank and I had grown increasingly upset by the care he was receiving at the rehab hospital. Unable to ring for nurses, he could go for hours in thirst or pain. At other times, his arm would numb up or his leg would feel like pins and needles. He was chastised for complaining, and while there were nurses who cared, there were also some who would let it be known they were burdened by his 'insatiable' needs. Frank's primary nurse thought it unwise to bring him home, the same nurse who took every opportunity to complain about the strain of having to move Frank about. I reasoned that at home I could take better care of him and get more sleep. We were both so sleep deprived. I decided I wanted him home.

A week before Thanksgiving, Frank came home to a makeshift bedroom in our dining room and an outdoor ramp we dubbed 'kamikaze' because it was short, steep and ended right in front of a huge maple tree. Later on, when Frank had a motorized wheel chair, he enjoyed the challenge of zooming down the ramp and stopping short, just before the tree. We cleared the dining room of my mother- in-law's hand-me-down table and chairs, a necessary task whose added benefit was to get rid of chairs I had always disliked. We set up the hospital bed, and began installing an accessible bathroom on the first floor.

At first we tried having a nighttime attendant, but this proved extremely disconcerting. We didn't have the option of interviewing or even meeting the attendants the health agency sent us. They usually showed up around 11 PM. I couldn't sleep, knowing there was a stranger in the house. Instead, I decided I would assist Frank myself. I moved a futon onto the floor next to Frank's hospital bed and slept there during the night. The disruption of having to get up during the night was countered by the peace of mind I enjoyed at not having total strangers revolving in and out of our home.

Our house became a beehive of activity. Having friends and family around kept us entertained and helped us avoid thinking about the long term implications of Frank's injury. I took a new job, working for the City of Chelsea. Because of near bankruptcy, the city had been placed in a legislatively-created receivership; the Receiver, Harry Spence, hired me as an Assistant Receiver to oversee human services for this small, beleaguered municipality. I could start part time and give myself a few months before moving up to full time. I loved the job, my colleagues, and the community, and remained there for six years. Chelsea provided me a respite away from the overwhelming demands at home. Still, by January I was juggling a full time job and my work at home.

Despite my relief at no longer having to interact with the hospital bureaucracy, there were times when I could feel my own unraveling, the burden, the widening disconnect between me and Frank, between me and myself. The sense of community support could not be sustained forever. Sooner or later, our friends would return to the vicissitudes of their own lives. Sooner or later, Frank and I would find ourselves together, alone. As the permanence of his diagnosis set in, our lives plunged to depths that frayed our bodies and debilitated our souls. Frank's physical pain was matched by depression and a sense of loss. As we worked for Frank to gain minimum control of his body, I felt I was losing control of my own.

It was possible to face the havoc Frank's wild nerves wrought: the steel belts that tightened around his waist; the pins and needles that pricked his deadened limbs. More difficult was the depression. Seeing Frank cry, out of the frustration of permanent dependency was more than I could bear – it tore at my heart. When friends insisted that I had to take care of myself, get more sleep, consider respite care, I'd look at them in disbelief – it was Frank who'd had the accident, not me. As the years went by, I realized they were right. My health was impaired – I wasn't sleeping. I developed an egg allergy and was one gigantic itch all over my body.

I was also becoming resentful, of what exactly, I wasn't sure: perhaps it was of fate, or of my friends who could so easily come and go, never stopping to consider their freedom; who would complain about seeming trivialities, failing to see that they were sailing on luxury crafts while we were groping for any old frayed rope. Perhaps it was Frank I resented, for having had the accident. Of course he hadn't planned it; still, if only he had been less of a daredevil, not always barreling through life. Then again, that was one of the things we all most admired about him - his passion for life.

Without mentioning it to Frank, I began to see a psychotherapist. I felt sneaky and guilty and confessed my therapy sessions to him a few weeks later. He was hurt that I hadn't said anything before. He said, "Why do you need to see someone? Why can't we talk about this together – we've always figured out our problems together. My condition doesn't lessen my ability to care or to problem solve. If we're going to get through this I've got to talk with you and you with me, not to someone else."

I said nothing, knowing that if I was truthful, I'd be hurtful. I'd have to say that I was tired of being a nursemaid, longed to have my dining room back and to sleep in my own bed upstairs, resented his accident and the stake it had driven into our life, wished for a fairy godmother who would grant me the sweetness of sleep. Why tell him? In the past, he would have been the first to know. I knew that even with his excruciating pain and depression, he was concerned about me. I knew there were nights when he lay awake in agony, watching the minute hand of the clock crawl its way around, but wouldn't call for me because he wanted to let me sleep. How could I add to his untenable burden?

Despite his pain, and emotional turmoil, Frank never stopped meeting with his students. He met with them when he was at the hospital. After he returned home, he was able to teach his classes at Boston University, with the assistance of Mary, his personal care attendant, [PCA], and a handicap-accessible van.

A word about Mary: We went through a number of personal care attendants who were provided by our private health insurance. But through the enlightened policy of Commonwealth Insurance, a state insurance policy available to disabled people, we were able to interview and hire our own attendant. In this way, we found Mary Rizzotto, a loving and lovely, intelligent, dedicated, fearless woman who became our friend and made it possible for us to begin building a new life.

Mary lived close by in Winthrop. She was with Frank for five years, five days a week, from eight in the morning until five in the evening. We made sure she took paid vacations, but other than vacation time away, she was absent no more than three or four days during that entire time. Frank considered her, not only his PCA and friend, but his student, taking opportunities to teach her things he knew about, like the computer or the van, and Mary was a quick and interested learner. The BU students and faculty all came to love her. We were also fortunate in finding Lynette, a friendly and diligent immigrant from Trinidad, who became our weekend PCA.

* * * *

One evening, after an especially exhausting day at BU, Frank accomplished a most incredible feat. He had been in great pain during the preceding days and, as a result, was over-medicated showing the symptoms of a drunk: bloodshot eyes, slurred speech, silly smile, falling asleep during dinner and afterward. I had tried keeping him awake on one of those evenings because he wanted to watch Benjamin Netanyahu be interviewed by Ted Koppel on Nightline. The next evening, a cold front came through the northeast and Frank's feet froze up, so much so that I had to give him a hot shower in the middle of the night. After that he fell asleep, only to wake me again in a state of panic. "You have to remove the ice cream from my feet," he told me. "The president announced on TV that if we remove the ice cream gradually, I won't feel the pain." "Go back to sleep," I answered un-amused. "You're hallucinating – I have to get some sleep or I'll be a basket case at work tomorrow."

The following evening, Frank was still heavily medicated, but we managed to watch the movie, "Up Close and Personal" on video cassette, and to have a pleasant evening. I prayed that he was through with his hallucinations and that the medication had stabilized. It hadn't. After going to bed, Frank began his bizarre, mind-altering adventure envisioning a cure for his paralysis. He imagined that I had double-clicked and dragged him to the computer desktop. (He had been immersed in learning a new voice-activated word processing program so computer jargon was heavily on his mind.) Dragged to the desktop, he was still paralyzed. Disappointed, he struggled and got his covers off. Noticing the wire that connected the electric blanket to the plug, he disconnected the plug from the socket, stuck it in his mouth and licked it. The mild shock, he thought, was exactly what he needed for the cure. Believing he was now able to walk, purposely and incredibly, he managed to move his entire body out of bed (a feat he could not have performed in his more lucid moments) only to land splattered on the floor. The evening ended as others had before, with my calling 911 and the paramedics helping me get Frank back into bed.

* * * *

In the early years, after Frank's return home, communicating with his students often fell to me. Frank would dictate and I would write, sometimes falling asleep over the computer. He would go to great lengths to explain what the student needed to do next on a paper. I felt sorry for some of the students, who were often told - emphatically and repeatedly - that their work needed improvement. I remember once saying to Frank, "You've already told this person three times that the paper is poor, I'm not going to write that again." He realized that his high standards were getting the better of him and stopped.

My role as a scribe ended when, after many trials and tribulations, Frank mastered the voice-activated word processing program. The technology was in its infancy and so there were many times when the program got stuck, frustrating Frank immensely. He was persistent, however, and before long he was effectively and independently using it. We all got a kick out of the commands that made letters appear and reappear, and whole paragraphs move up and down. My only regret was that his students would once again suffer his exacting ways. Even so, a handful made it onto the graduation stage receiving doctoral degrees. These were highly emotional scenes, Frank wearing his cap and gown, hooding his students while seated in his wheel chair.

FRANK, JAY AND AURA, DECEMBER 28, 1992, PART 1: "IN THE PAST, FRANK WOULD TAKE OVER FOR ME"

Jay: It strikes me that the two of you don't have a lot of time to yourselves. It's action time when you have it, for much of the day. There are people coming in and out and there are phone calls, so you really don't have the kind of time that apparently you had this afternoon, where you were able just to talk.

Frank: We don't have relaxing time. Partly because usually, there is so much to do. For Aura, she has eight things to do, all of which need to be done right away. I mean *need* to be done right away. My pills need to be in order. I need to eat. I need to get cleaned up.

(Aura joins the conversation after a phone call with a friend who is organizing Frank's night-time care givers.)

Jay: We were just talking about the fact that your time together this afternoon was a rare thing. Most of the time you're doing this and that, filling out the list and the pills and all the things you have to do—

Aura: —the pills, that's right.

Jay: —and all the other things that have to happen. So that you really don't get time when you can just relax and talk very often.

Aura: That's true.

Jay: Plus the fact that people are coming in and out all the time, and the phone's ringing.

Aura: It's constant. It's constant. It's always something going on.

Frank: But that activity, in a way, has saved us. I mean it's killed us and it's saved us. It's an Everest/Death Valley thing, because people coming in, us girding up and being hospitable, means other people to talk to about my pain rather than just talking to Aura and the kids. Other people to smooth out my hands or rub my feet. Other people to turn the television off or do this or do that.

Jay: Sure, but maybe there's a way to have both, because it really strikes me that you do need time, just time.

Aura: Yeah, I think that it's had a negative and a positive effect. The positive effect has been that because people are coming, not to be hosted or to be company, I can say, "Do you want coffee or tea"—usually they come laden with stuff—but I don't have to play that role of hostess. It's okay for me to have this kitchen that is falling apart or the unfinished bathroom; it all makes sense; it's all easily explainable.

Remember that night when Frank L. came over to be interviewed for a job as an aide and Mark Weiner was here and Dan Manning and Gail and Connell Foley [students, colleagues and neighbors]? And John Moore [contractor] was in there, banging away with one of his assistants. There was a real feeling of energy. I was trying to be sociable; talking to Dan, finding out how GBLS [Greater Boston Legal Services, which Dan directed and where Aura had worked] was, and at the same time interviewing Frank L., because it was the first time I had met him. It was very awkward. How do you interview someone? What kind of a typing test do I give him? Do I ask him to raise Frank's legs and straighten out his hands?

But it hit me that amidst all that stuff there was a feeling of—I kept thinking of what it must have been like in the old socialist communities of the eighteen hundreds. (laughs) Somehow I felt like I was a part of that. All these people, coming and going, were part of this community, and I was not playing the role of host, which was very nice. So that was the positive part.

Jay: There's something very truth-bearing about all of that. With Al's comment that Frank is more Frank than he ever was, it's like there's this giant eraser that's getting rid of anything superficial or contrived and getting down to the bare bones, the essentials of living.

Aura: I just kept thinking, it's like getting together to build a barn. Everyone comes over and brings food, but there's a mission: it's one mission and everyone is working towards it and for it. It was partly that the wood stove was burning, that there was a cozy feeling. (to Frank who occasionally dozes off during the conversation) Stop falling asleep when I talk! So it was part of that.

But I think the downside for me is that I feel like I have no control of my life. Frank is really grasping for control and demanding control—"Do this" and "Do that"; for obvious reasons, he needs it. I feel that there's this inverse correlation, between his trying to gain control, minimal, minimal control that he needs, and my having no control any more. I get up in the morning and before I even have a cup of coffee, which is usually critical for me, I'm kind of on. It's not just with one task; it's usually with three or four tasks. And before I know it, like this morning, the doctor is ringing the doorbell and Frank is sitting on the commode, or James [aide] is coming in, and Bob Archer and Shanti [friends] show up from Amherst, and I'm telling them, "Come on in to the kitchen. (laughs) But Frank is sitting on the commode, so Shanti, you can't look, but Bob can", making a joke of it.

The phone is ringing. Then the plumbers have come in and I'm supposed to tell them that they've basically screwed up, because they didn't put in the right faucet, and I'm thinking that the radiator doesn't work. I'm trying to figure out how to go out and do the banking because Dylan has given me a thousand dollar check and we just got the IRA check; I've got to pay the credit line. And there are all these groceries that have to be bought.

And I feel like I don't have any control. Tonight I thought it would be nice to go to yoga and I could have just walked out and gone. But then the neurotic part of me, as Frank points out and Dylan points out, says "You can't leave." Why do I have to do all the dishes? Can't I just leave a message for others to do them? I don't know what that's apropos of.

Jay: It's apropos of exactly where you started. You, too, need your boundaries, your control. The scene you described of this morning is humorous, but it's also a nightmare.

Aura: And it's typical.

Jay: Have you touched base with what's-her-name?

Aura: Sonya? [therapist] I did. I'm going to see her January 8th. Frank doesn't even know this. To give you an example of a relationship that's taken a detour.

Frank: Who's Sonya?

Aura: Yeah, who's Sonya? So Jay knows who Sonya is and Jay and I had this long discussion about whether I was going to see her. It was something I just figured, why tell Frank. Is he going to feel bad about it, or is he going to not focus on it, or is he going to think that, somehow, he's responsible.

Jay: That very issue is so important. I hear your reluctance to bring out your needs, which are not oppositional to, but very different from Frank's needs; and because of the time factor, they do oppose Frank's needs. To get that opposition out where it's visible and accepted, it's a natural thing in a situation like this, it seems to me. It makes it easier for you to say, "I have these things I need to do for myself. At times, Frank, you say, as you did that night, "I'd like Aura to have a good night's sleep, so let's not bother her."

It's not like Frank's unaware of that, but it needs to be almost as visible as this schedule (points to schedule on blackboard in the kitchen) which is for Frank's needs. Not that it isn't for your needs, but it's focused on Frank. There needs to be something that is focused on you. In a sense, Frank has fewer problems; when he has a need, he lets it be known, whereas with you, the pressure has to build somewhat.

Aura: I think that's true. I think that's what Frank was saying before; that rather than calling Nancy [a visiting friend] to help, I just move the bed.

Jay: I think you're going to have to work at that.

(The conversation turns to Aura's decision to see a therapist, then to ways of monitoring phone calls to cut down on interruptions)

Aura: Well, we should probably finish this train of thought.

Jay: It has to do with two themes: one is both of you having time together, as you did today. Also, your needs [Frank] being in tension with your needs [Aura]. It's that way. And the only way to deal with that tension is to acknowledge it.

Aura: What I find interesting is that as the day wears on, my whole attitude changes. It starts out in the morning, when I'm too out of it to really function and feeling like I need to start functioning right away. Then, once I'm awake, I'm fine. And then, all of a sudden, I find, nighttime comes on. And the idea of doing one more thing—like last night, you wanted to shower; and yet you [Frank] knew. You said, "Oh, no, you're too tired." You even had the conversation with the nurse about it. And you thought, well, maybe Anelisa could help, or tonight, you thought maybe Jay could get you into the shower. Frank is well aware, because he knows me, that there is a certain hour when I just can't function.

And yet often I find that I am functioning well beyond that hour and I get really irritable, like "Don't ask me to do this."

Jay: What would it be like for you to make a list of the things you need? Just to get them down so that they are as concrete as the electrician's list or the list of things to be done.

Frank: It would be too long. You'd run out of paper.

Aura: Well one thing, I just wish that when I started something, I could see it through to the end. I mean, that frustrates the hell out of me. I'll be trying to do the checks and—not even things for myself—I can't tell you the last time I read a newspaper or a book. I did manage to go to yoga a couple of weeks ago ... I'm pretty compulsive. Dylan says to Frank, and he says to me, "There are certain things you just have to put aside, now." I haven't been able to do that, so I try very hard to get little tasks done and I don't succeed. Dylan will come down and find me sweeping and doing the dishes and he accuses me of liking it, because why am I doing it.

In the past, Frank would take over for me. He'd say to me, "I'll finish that." Or "We'll do it together." Or "I'll help you do that, go upstairs for a rest. So now you're [Frank] not being there. I don't know—it's part of what I was saying to Frank the other day. It's coupled with the loss of the relationship. That was what was so great about this afternoon: it was a recapture of—if Frank will recognize or acknowledge, like he has, "You're doing a million things"—in a way, that's a lot of it. Then you say, 'Okay', at least there's an acknowledgment; but without the acknowledgment, it makes it all the harder.

Jay: In addition to the exercises by which you [Frank] regain your walking, you both have to have a structure by which you regain time to be together without having to do other things.

Frank: I have to—

Aura: Lie down.

Frank: Or maybe take a shower.

Jay: Speaking of which, it's 10:15 (PM), and I'll take over.

BOUNDARIES - JAY

At first
I shrank
when nurses came
to help

I didn't want
to raid your space,
cross boundaries
breached
by injury's invasion

in time
I saw
that you required
more care
than help-worn nurses
could provide

sensed
that you accepted
parted curtains
in your life

Jay Clark and Aura Sanchez Garfunkel

I eased
toward intimate logistics
holding a glass
while you sipped
proffering a dish
when, teeth brushed,
you spat
helping nurses
turn you in the bed

once
you sneezed
and,
teetered at privacy's gate,
I said,
(knowing you couldn't
hold a handkerchief),
I could blow your nose

you said
with a smile
to smooth the path
through intimacy's underbrush,
Wait a minute
We didn't write that into the contract
We said you could come as many times as you want
But you can't blow my fucking nose

we laughed

so I knew
that boundaries
still endured

when you went home
exchanging
call buttons
and staff visits
for processions
of doubtful aides
I became a certain companion
one night a week

nurses absent
I enlarged
the realm of my assistance
rustling midnight snacks
tucking you in
dressing and undressing you
emptying the urinal

arriving at your house
I'd deem it less intrusive
to walk right in
than to ring the bell

so it went for many months,
till nascent order
bred routines
and you
could manage
on your own
without
a nighttime guest

relief was
mixed
no more drives home
in early morning daze

yet I felt
the end
of darkness intimacy
you-and-me alone
in vastness

a closeness
forged
in fire

normalcy
brought
day visits

parted curtains
closed around you

I rang
the bell
and someone
let me in

FRANK AND JAY, MONDAY, DECEMBER 28, 1992, PART 2: "I SUDDENLY BECAME A BORN-AGAIN EXERCISER"

Jay: We had a shower and we're continuing. Remarkable shower. Frank is now sitting on the bed before going off to sleep. There are still items to cover. Including hallucinogenic states—I forget what the other was.

Frank: Well, it will come up. What I'd like to do is chronicle the last week and then concentrate on these topics.

The week was characterized by extreme Mount Everest ups and Death Valley downs. The downs included times when I was in excruciating pain for hours at a time. They included a five-hour afternoon session, in which one of our workers, Cindy, spent the time with me and anything she did—massage or working my legs or my arms or my hands or holding me—seemed to cause me more rather than less pain.

In an all-night session with Jay and subsequent sessions with others staying overnight different things got built in, like having tea and going into the kitchen and having a cookie, sitting on the side of the bed, listening to music. Sometimes we would talk about other things: anecdotes about our previous lives together, our husbands, our wives, our children. But they were characterized by an almost unending focus on pain. During this period, I developed a swallowing problem.

Jay: Oh, I didn't know that.

Frank: I couldn't swallow, maybe four or five gulps and I would be locked. I'd be gasping. I could breathe through my nose and mouth, but I couldn't swallow food. After a few days I could swallow Jell-O. So I had a severe swallowing problem. Every time I began to doze off, I would start gasping and wake up. In seeking help from David [MD] and the nurses, I discussed with them whether it was medication or anxiety related, or whether it was something else. I was afraid that I had developed a permanent muscular throat problem and it was a spinal problem. And that—

Jay: —you were losing rather than gaining.

Frank: No one could suggest anything to do about it. In fact, I couldn't even describe it to people; they would keep on asking, "When do you do it and under what conditions?" Just the verbal description was enormously difficult. But it was clear to anyone who was with me that I couldn't swallow.

The eating problem went on longer—four or five days. When I put stuff in my mouth, I would have to spit it out; I couldn't swallow anything but Jell-O. I could take in milk through a straw. I could continue to swallow pills by taking a sip of fluid with a straw, but I couldn't take them the other way. There were so many problems and possibilities in that week; eating, breathing, sleeping—there was one forty-eight hour period where I don't think I slept five minutes.

Then a strange thing happened. It was three or four in the morning and I was having the swallowing problem and no one knew what to do about it, when Seth came in to stay with me for a while. Somehow it occurred to me that when I had a sore throat, I [would take] a lozenge to ease the soreness of the throat and make it easier to swallow. So I said to Seth, "Do you have any hard candies?" Seth said, "What's a hard candy?" We resolved the communication problem and he went to the Christmas candies and found a little piece of peppermint candy. I stuck it in my mouth and the swallowing problem disappeared. As long as I had a hard candy stuck in my mouth, I no longer had a swallowing problem.

Jay: Was that associated with the nausea, you experienced?

Frank: (laughs) I forgot that one.

Jay: I don't want to leave any pain out of the picture!

Frank: Yeah. I also had a twenty-four hour period of nausea and nearly throwing up.

Jay: Yeah, I spent part of that holding the bowl for you.

Frank: On the other hand, I experienced some tremendous gains in my walking ability, balancing, and handling a hospital bed, doing something other than simply lying in it or rattling the sides of it. Those Mount Everest highs were extraordinary, going through terrible things and then having great gains.

Jay: I came over Christmas Eve Day, and you had had two horrendous nights, and then you had this miraculous walking. Phenomenal.

Frank: That pattern existed throughout the week. It consisted of so many rich, valuable things—with the kids, with Aura, with friends. My pattern during the night, when I went through these very painful periods, would generally be to moan and groan, talk all night to Al and you and Aura, ask to be turned around, or get a drink of this or that.

With Aura, one night I just continued—it may have been every five minutes although to me it felt like hours—asking her to get me a drink or take the covers off or put them aside or let me stand at the side of the bed. Finally, in despair, she stuck me on my back, shut out the lights and said, "I'm going to sleep." I lay there, again for what I thought was an hour; probably it was a minute or two. And then I shrieked out that I couldn't stand it; I was too hot. She got up and opened the window and went to bed. I lasted another two minutes and then I shrieked again; she said that she needed to sleep and I should go to sleep. I told her I couldn't go to sleep just because someone asked me to go to sleep. Meanwhile, I hadn't slept for days. We could say, as we talked and despaired throughout the night, that we were both right. There was nothing we could do about it. Somehow, we made it through that night.

Jay: Sounds like the night of nights. That was the night before Christmas Eve, because I came over that noon.

Frank: This was followed by my becoming more independent on the walker. I began to see a time, concretely, when I would be walking again. Sometime during that second week, I decided that I was going to exercise. But I didn't know how to exercise in bed. They [therapists] did their little foot-raisings, but you can only do a few of those and then you are bored or all worn out. I would mostly get passive exercises, where someone would push my leg back and forth or begin shaping my hand. In a conversation with a couple of therapists, I heard their litany about how passive therapy is no good; it has to be active: you should be eating, you should be doing your exercises, not someone else for you. I suddenly became a born-again exerciser.

I've never been an exerciser. I can't jog; I can't do anything repetitive; I can't do sit-ups. The only thing I can do is stretch before I play squash. I've always had to be involved in something competitive like tennis or squash—years ago I was always involved with basketball—always sports, competitive sports, racquet sports. Suddenly I got the feeling that exercise was the only way out of the drug cycle. In spite of my years of experience about drugs, questioning their validity, use and dependency, I had become totally enmeshed in drug thinking: when my muscles got stiff, I would think, "What's the drug for softening up your muscles"; when I got depressed, I'd think of what is the antidepressant; when I went into pain, I would say, 'What's the drug to deal with pain?'; when I had my throat problem I thought, "Okay, what can I take for it?"

I don't know exactly how it evolved, but exercise became the way to do something other than to take drugs. It became something to control body temperature, something to do in those endless hours when I couldn't sleep, a way of being active rather than passive.

Jay: Sounds like a real epiphany. You came into this crisis and then, somehow, you went through to the other side of it.

Frank: I had received messages that exercise would play a role in this, but no one ever told me that the way to fight pain was to exercise.

(Aura comes in; Jay tells her he can stay late in the morning. Aura needs to give Frank a suppository; Jay offers, but Frank wants Aura to do it. They tell Jay that Frank is free of side effects, after coming off a medication that made his speech slurred and labored.)

Jay: (resuming after Aura leaves) So, you were saying that you discovered active exercise and you're doing that now.

Frank: Not only did I do it, but I went into an exercise *frenzy*. I got the idea that the way to beat the drug thing was, first of all, to get rid of the pain pills. They were the stumbling blocks that set the whole cycle down: the pain pills lead to tremendous stiffness, temporary paralysis; they lead to a state where you can't do anything for yourself.

So I said to myself, or maybe I didn't, but I started acting as if the way to deal with pain was to exercise—keep your body moving in any way that you could. Since I have only one good arm, that limits what I can do. Many nights, my legs would be stiff, sometimes more than stiff; they just wouldn't move. Sometimes I could only exercise my upper body, my right arm; limited exercise with my left arm. And I would do this for four or five hours at a stretch, sometimes eight hours. Perpetually. Whenever I felt anything like a cramp coming on, I would do it. When I went to sleep, I would do it because it was a way to get to sleep, though generally the exercise would so tense me up, I couldn't sleep. So it could defeat the purpose; but then, I wasn't waiting all night to get comfortable or to go to sleep.

Jay: What about the pain? Did it reduce the pain?

Frank: The pain went away. There was discomfort; there was exhaustion; stomach and swallowing problems developed; but that pain, which had so engulfed and swept me, inside my legs, inside my thighs and arms—disappeared. I was still uncomfortable and aching but — (Aura comes in with Frank's medication)

Jay: These two white pills are what?

Aura: That's the Backlafan and that's the muscle relaxant. It should alleviate all that spasming he's had—okay, I'll see you both in the morning. Call me in the night if you need me.

Jay: Okay. Sleep well.

Aura: Actually, I will. (Aura leaves, Frank and Jay resume.)

Jay: You've told your system, "I'm going to take care of you with exercise and I want you to calm down with the pain", and it's worked.

Frank: Different techniques come into play at different stages. At one stage I was using the class of activities which we might call mental activities, like self hypnosis, imagery and relaxation. You've always encouraged me to explore those and Aura has encouraged me, and been involved in mental activities in her study and reading. They were very successful, in that I was able to relax different parts of my body and literally feel the pins and needles going down my arms into my hands. That helped me get some sleep and calm down, early in my experience at the rehab hospital.

But then, I listened to a relaxation tape where the narrator is telling you to, for example, take your forehead and show tension, then relax it and note the difference; show anger with your teeth, then relax; they do these contrasts with your eyes, nose and mouth. It just turned me off; I thought it was somewhat ludicrous. At a later stage when I was going through some real tough stuff at the hospital, Aura tried some imaging with me and it just didn't work. The breathing to control pain that you tried with me; I tried it. But it seemed as if the problems I was having were at one level, and this was at another level. Something like that had worked weeks before, but this time it didn't work.

Jay: That makes sense.

Frank: Yeah, so I've been getting away from it. I also recognize that one of the ways I have dealt with problems before, over the years, has been athletically—climbing mountains or exhaustive skiing in very cold weather; a lot of things where they're punishing, and I find them very enjoyable. They're activity-oriented. You do things with people; that's the way you talk with them and relate to them. Sometimes you don't talk, you just do things with them. So the exercise really—

Jay: —was *doing.*

Frank: —was doing. For four or five days, I beat the pain, which meant I didn't have to take the —

Jay: —Atavan?

Frank: —no, no not the Atavan, what I call the V pill.

One of the facts about this whole thing is, I'm taking all these drugs over and over again; people are mentioning their names and—

Jay: —Vicidan—

Frank: —yeah, Vicidan—and I cannot remember a single name. In order to communicate, I do remember the first letters; I call them the V pill and the B pill. When I talk with people who know about drugs—who spout the names—I know that, cognitively, I've got this problem; and yet, I have to talk about the drugs because we're discussing them all the time. Somehow, I'm trying to keep them away by not knowing their names.

Jay: That's all right. Good thing.

Frank: I got away from the painkiller, which meant I didn't have these totally-engulfing drug stiffness mornings. I could get more out of the therapy sessions and talk to people, think less about myself, and more about other people's issues and problems.

Aura would be in bed and I would be exercising for five hours, making a terrible racket. It's very noisy exercise, because you're rattling at the cage, rattling your bars, and you're up and down on the bed, twisting and turning. And yet Aura said she slept right through it. So it accomplished the purpose of letting her sleep and keeping me busy. I didn't have to worry about time elapsed, waiting to go to sleep.

I realized, also, that I couldn't sleep with covers on; once I got the covers on, I couldn't move my legs. The exercising permitted me to be in bed all night without having covers on; also I discovered that an electric blanket underneath could serve as a way of not having covers on, but still getting heat. So I began the exercising, sleeping without covers, having something to do all night. The pain was gone, that kind of pain.

It was so different from the way I had dealt with it with Al, with you, with Aura, with Cindy. But it also had other consequences, like the pain often being on top of my left arm. My left arm seemed like it was going backwards, getting stiffer and stiffer. I can't even lift it up today; I can't even beat gravity. My right arm, which was really involved in most of the exercise, seemed to be getting stronger and stronger, and maintaining or getting further range of action.

Jay: Can you move your wrist at all?

Frank: In my right arm, yeah.

Jay: Is that a new thing?

Frank: I've had that for quite a while. I can make a fist. I could control the fist. I have a pretty strong grip now; it's slowly getting stronger.

Jay: Are you at a point where having a nerf ball would help your grip, if not your finger dexterity?

Frank: Nah. What I need, I think, maybe four times a day, is for people to really spread my fingers out, really give my hand a going over, although that's passive. I've kind of rejected almost all the passive stuff, but with the hands—I think it's like what I said about visualization, at certain stages certain kinds of things come into play; at other times they don't. With the passive exercises, I wasn't exercising all of my body. Some parts were getting nothing, and some were getting an excessive amount of action, like my right arm. That seemed to me to be against this new set of principles I've found.

I started by letting myself go down on the bed; usually it was accidental. I suddenly began to find new positions in the bed. And this is tied up with dependency; I'm so totally dependent. I always have to ask people to do things for me. Your relationship with friends, with acquaintances, with family, with people you've known a month, with people you've known your whole life, changes into a total dependency relationship. Well, not totally, because —

Jay: —you've got to teach them. (chuckles)

Frank: Yeah, it's much more confused than that.

Well, by moving around in the bed, and the exercises, and not having to call someone, slowly I became—I don't know if it is safe to say—creative; or serendipitous. I'd suddenly be in a position in which I could exercise a different part of my body: my arm in a different way; get my leg over one of the bars and shake it up and down. That dealt with the problem that, with spinal cord pain, a lot of exercising is almost impossible to do, even if you wanted to.

So I would go frantically, night after night, not sleeping, and this culminated on Saturday night. That afternoon I'd been having a very pleasant time, people were here, and I had done some great walking. But then I got cold and stiff, and I got frantic that I was losing it. I started exercising at four in the afternoon and continued without stopping until nine or ten. Within these four or five hours, I got some help from Aura and Anelisa. I started doing whatever I could do with my foot, thigh, arm, going back and forth. I hadn't slept for forty-eight hours before that; about ten o'clock I went to sleep and slept for about seven or eight hours. When I was going to sleep I relaxed; I'm pretty sure I had a shower. The introduction of the shower for the first time at home—as the first floor bathroom was completed—is a very important part of the story.

When I went to sleep, I was already so stiff that I could hardly move either leg; my left arm was totally paralyzed and my right had lost functioning tremendously, or so it seemed. I had a terrible nightmare that I couldn't urinate: I was getting more and more pressure and I was about to blow up. The lack of the ability to urinate was going to kill me. So when I woke up about three, I couldn't move, and I woke Aura up. I was convinced that I'd never walk again. I thought that I might not even live beyond that morning. (Anelisa passes through) Hi, honey.

Anelisa: Isn't it well past your bedtime?

Frank: Yeah, it sure is. Isn't it past your bedtime?

Anelisa: Nope.

Frank: Did you have a nice evening?

Anelisa: Yeah.

Frank: (resuming) So the next morning was incredible among incredible experiences; I was totally convinced that I had lost the battle. I couldn't uncross my legs. At one point, Aura was leaning on me and I looked at her, and said, "Oh, God! It's happened to her, too." I was convinced that she was gone—

Jay: —paralyzed, or dead, or both—

Frank: —both. She was just there, and she was looking at me. Later, when we talked about it, Aura said yes, she was there and she was leaning on me; her interpretation of it was that she was just collecting her energy. But I didn't see it that way at all. Then Rose (aide) came, and she couldn't even move me.

Jay: That was this morning, wasn't it?

Frank: Yeah. I just looked at them and wondered why they were—in fact, I was surprised that Aura got up and started talking about coffee, because I thought she was—

Jay: —dead?

Frank: Dead. Then I was really surprised when she talked about putting a suppository in me. I said, "God! What good is that? I don't need a suppository. It will just mean shit all over a dead man." I hardly talked to them for an hour or two.

Finally, when they said they were going to put me on the commode, I said, "Okay, but I can't stand up." They got out a transfer board and dragged me onto the commode. I couldn't figure out what they were doing; what did I have to go to the bathroom for? Rose kept saying, "Come on, lift that leg," and I thought it was stupid; it didn't make any sense. They were talking about what did I want for breakfast.

I did get on the commode and when I was sitting there, all kinds of activities started in the house. The therapist came. Friends of ours from Amherst came. Aura was talking with them as if everything was normal: "Frank's a little bit under the weather this morning."

So, I'm sitting there on the commode and I lifted my leg. I said, "What the hell am I lifting my leg for?" I moved my toes, lifted the other leg, pulled up one sock, pulled up the other. None of it made any sense. By the time I got ready to get off the commode, I realized that my expectations about what was going to happen were somewhat off. I didn't know that they were totally off at the time. I hadn't told anyone that I thought I would never walk again.

Then I was able to stand to get off the commode. And I actually walked after that, with the therapist. I did some things during the walking that were kind of extraordinary for me in terms of the amount of independence, which you saw a little of later today.

Jay: That's quite a story; it rivals the ordeal of Odysseus. It's a saga coming to a point where it looks as if you've crossed the River Lethe. Then you discover you haven't crossed the river, though it seemed as if you had. It's different from some other people's description of near-death experiences, where they see white lights, but that's what you had, a psychological near-death experience.

Then you come through this, and your functioning comes back, and there it is, gently but firmly confronting the notion that you're paralyzed and you're dead and you're through.

Frank: The night before, sometime during that exercise period between four and nine, I told Aura I wanted to speak to the nurse or the doctor, so I spoke [by phone] to Jean, the nurse on duty. I told her what had happened the coldness, stiffness, and fear of paralysis, and she said, "Well, I just think it's the result of all the exercise you had." So, the message was clearly there. The data, the epiphany was there.

Rendezvous - Jay

Sometimes
amid myriad tasks
they shared
their lives
with me
a mountain meeting

an exhalation
of exertion's breath
theirs' to live
mine to ease their night

the summit
their constant home
a place
of piercing vision

unplanned
we gathered
each of us a traveler
on unsought heights
I a visitor
to their aerie

it seemed
as if
we'd
dwelt
for ages
in that spot
just us
against enormity

for moments
humor and perspective
made trial smaller
less fierce
before
the next night came

PART V. RETROSPECTIVE

SNOW WALK - JAY

Frank and I
set forth
in winter
he on wheels,
I on foot

he speeds ahead
I run
he brakes
the wheelchair spins and skids

eyes agleam,
in snow bank
he awaits
my arrival

I pull him out
and he renews
his rush
toward fate's
next challenge

wild boy
mad scientist

Jay Clark and Aura Sanchez Garfunkel

he's discovered
a new test
of friction's laws

turns
outing
into escapade,
his dance
with life

AURA'S PERSPECTIVE:
REGENERATION

Slowly, with help from friends and family and more effective medication, Frank and I began to crawl out of our abyss, to create a new, albeit circumscribed, life. As I look back, I realize that until then we had fallen into a survival mode. We had lost the ability to dream about a future - understandable, as the future looked as grim as the present. The Buddhists say that we spend too much of our time thinking about the past or the future; that we have to live in-the-moment. I believe that is true, but there is also something to be said for making plans, even if it's only to say that next year, you'll take a trip to visit friends, or next week, you'll go to dinner and take in a movie, buy a new living room couch. For us, all that ordinary planning had stopped. If we made it through the night with Frank's nerves not taunting him and we could sleep for 3 or 4 hours without interruption, well, that was cause for celebration. When we finally discovered Elevil, an anti-depressant medication that brought Frank great pain relief, we were able to reintroduce 'future' to our lives. We were ecstatic with the respite that Elevil brought. Frank's natural exuberance re-emerged. After many visits to specialists and many hours of physical therapy, Frank had come to accept that he would never walk independently again; with Elevil, however, his wheel chair world expanded.

At home, we were faced with living in an old New England home that was in no way accessible. We looked into apartments at Harbor Towers and discussed moving to the yet-to-be-built Cambridge Co-housing. But the possibilities were depressing, as we loved our home in Winthrop and didn't really want to leave it. I started to envision what we would need in order to make it more navigable for Frank and we agreed to give it a try. We installed a mini-elevator, said good-bye to the kamikazi ramp and constructed a 'real' ramp, remodeled the kitchen, and purchased a wheel chair accessible van. The elevator allowed both Frank and me to go back to sleeping on the second floor. We enlarged one room by tearing down a wall allowing space for the hospital bed. With our dining room once again a dining room, we could return to having our large Christmas and Passover celebrations. The van, of course, allowed Frank to travel with his motorized chair, getting in and out with minimal assistance. His dream was that someday, he'd be able to drive the van himself.

My son Dylan, visiting from Olympia, WA, where he was now studying, suggested we apply for an assist dog. Frank was skeptical and didn't give it much thought, even though he was a dog lover. I decided to look into it and applied to NEADS, (National Education for Assistance Dog Services), in Boylston, Massachusetts. I had heard that people were often on waiting lists for assist dogs for years. For whatever reason, we were lucky. They got in touch with us soon after we applied and in less than a year we had been awarded Truman, the sweetest, most beautiful, two year old black Lab.

When we went for our interview, the NEADS staff members who interviewed us concluded that Frank was a reserved and gentle sort of man (they were dead wrong of course). The two dog trainers had brought in Lucas, a chocolate lab, to give Frank a feel for the dogs and the training Frank would be required to undergo. They kept instructing Frank to encourage Lucas by saying 'good boy' whenever Lucas obeyed a command. Frank, who was not about to be told how to talk to a dog, or anyone for that matter, resisted their instruction, every now and then reluctantly acquiescing with an 'attaboy'. The trainers confused Frank's intractability for shyness or reserve. The misperception was fortunate as they paired him up with a very gentle and polite dog. Frank was ecstatic when he met Truman. He knew immediately that Truman was a very special animal and I believe he grew to love him at once, as did the rest of our family. Truman changed Frank profoundly. Even in the throes of depression or pain, being with Truman made him happy. They were the best of buddies, Truman going wherever Frank went. If he had to observe a student in a student teaching placement, Truman would accompany him, often playing the role of icebreaker. Children especially, who might be reluctant to approach a person in a wheel chair, would not hesitate to come up to Frank and ask if they could pet his dog. Because of the Americans With Disabilities Act, Truman - a service dog - was allowed to go wherever Frank went. We were given seats on planes with enough room to accommodate Truman at our feet.

With Frank's pain in abeyance, we began to regain control of our lives; began to dream again. Because Frank had been a sports enthusiast before the accident we decided to look into adaptive sports. He started taking adaptive skiing lessons at Sunapee Mountain in New Hampshire and sailing lessons at Shake-A-Leg, a boating organization on Narragansett Bay, Rhode Island, for disabled people. I was amazed at how many impaired people continued to live athletic lives with the help of adaptive technologies. These ventures back into the sporting world were full of trepidation. Getting the adapted skis - a chair on a pair of skis - on the chair lift was a major undertaking. Sometimes it failed and Frank would be thrown off onto his helmeted head before the lift took off. Refusing to be intimidated Frank was always ready to try again, knowing that once up on the mountain the excitement of going down would give his trapped body an exhilarating sense of freedom.

Perhaps the most precious by-product of Frank's dependency was that our children, young adults in their late teens and early twenties, became closer to each other and to us; all but his son Max that is. Max, then in his thirties, was living in Boston at the time. (A giant rift in Frank and Max's relationship, stemming back to Max's early teen years, had caused a continued estrangement between him and the rest of us.) Reshaping our relationships to one another was among the many unanticipated difficulties created by Frank's paralysis. There were major blow-ups that often reduced us all to tears, even as they were weaving us into a tighter weft.

Dylan, being the oldest in our household, and Frank's step-son, became more protective and defensive of me. He was concerned that, as a result of my care for Frank, my own health was suffering and that I was always exhausted. He resented Frank's burden on me. When Frank became overly demanding, he'd call him on it. Having no other choice than to rely on our help, there were many times when Frank would say, "give me this", or "get me that". This would irk Dylan, who thought Frank should say 'please' when he asked for things. Finally, he said as much to Frank. Frank retorted that it wasn't a situation where 'please' was in order: when you're drowning, and a passerby is near, you don't say 'please' can you save me. Or, 'please' can you open a safety net for me so that I don't burn to death. This wasn't a question of ingratitude or entitlement – it was a matter of survival. It was a profound statement that I don't think any of us got at the time. Paradoxically, through this struggle and in a sense, tug-of-war, with me being the rope, he and Frank became closer. Frank realized that Dylan was now an adult; he began to talk to him as an adult, about his schooling, about outdoor sports, about traveling. He saw how much they had in common, how much his own love of the outdoors had influenced Dylan's. He also saw how much Dylan was doing to help out. Dylan realized that he could speak his mind to Frank, and neither he nor Frank would fall apart.

Frank's relationship with Seth also had to be re-shaped. Seth was living on the west coast. He had quit Boston University, a semester shy of graduating, determined to get out of Winthrop. There was a rather stultifying life-style among young adults in the town – one that over-valued the weekend with its drinking and partying - and he wanted to get away from it. This all happened a few years before Frank's accident. Frank was sad that he hadn't finished college.

At first, Seth worked out on a ranch in Nevada. Later, he moved to Santa Barbara, where he worked and went to acting school. We had friends in Santa Barbara who looked out for him and helped Frank come around to accepting Seth's departure. A few years after the injury, we visited Seth in Santa Barbara and ended up falling in love with the city. Eventually we realized that Seth was in a much better place there, emotionally and physically, than he had been at home.

Frank and Seth shared a love of sports. During every important game - and let's face it, aren't they all 'important' - Seth would call and they'd watch the game together, long distance. No sooner did something extraordinary happen in the ever 'important' game than the phone was ringing and the house was filled with transcontinental screams of joy over the home run, the goal, or the touch down that had been scored. Sometimes calls came in from all three kids. In the past, I had found such exuberance over a game ridiculous. Now I treasured it. For Frank's sake, I looked forward to these enthusiastic phone calls.

As for Anelisa, after her recovery from her jaw surgery, she moved into a dorm at BU. She was close by and came home frequently. She remembers that there was now quality time to talk with her father. Before the accident, he had been a doer, always active and busy. He loved being with the kids but it was focused around an activity: playing basketball; helping to make a table; taking the boat out. Now there was time to tell stories and get to know each other in a different way. She learned about Frank's adventurous and iconoclastic past; about his bicycling in the Alps with a gearless bike, collapsing into France; about his ascending to the presidency of the newly-formed faculty union at Boston University and taking on the autocratic President Silber; about his being arrested in Mississippi in the mid-60's for daring to frequent a local white establishment with local blacks. And Frank learned about who his children were becoming. He needed his family in a way that he had not before his accident. Thus, the kids were promoted from the status of dependents to responsible young adults we both desperately needed to lean on.

Jay Clark and Aura Sanchez Garfunkel

Frank and Truman, Assist Dog Graduation, 1997

Don Friedman, Aura and Frank, Franconia, NH, 1994

Frank at Shake-a-Leg, Newport, RI, 1998

Frank skiing at Mt. Sunapee, 1998

If I'm Around - Jay

Off to Belle Isle
in the van
that November day
nine years since

somehow, locking his chair
I'd pinched his finger
I drove off
with guilt
increased
because he'd not complained

ten minutes on
surrounded by tall grasses
a few birds
Belle Isle Inlet
and November stillness
the three of us
headed toward
the bay,
Truman padding along
consulting innumerable smells,
Frank going full throttle
along the path

I running to catch up

Frank asked me
to throw Truman's ball
away from water
Next time we'll
let him go in, if I'm around.

I didn't heed his words
though I recalled them
five days later when he died

did premonition shape his words,
a signal unreceived by me;
or did he speak
not sensing crouching truth?

the moment was obscured
by Frank's off-path plunging
into rush and muck
to see how close to water
he could press
'til he'd get stuck
and I'd haul him back
to firmer ground

who'd see
eternity's blink
roughing it
with a friend
in the marshes of Belle Isle

AURA'S PERSPECTIVE:
RENAISSANCE

As part of our renaissance, Frank and I began to travel again. On a visit to see Dylan in Olympia, we took a side trip to the Olympic Peninsula. We marveled at Northwest forests, so different from New England's, with giant redwoods, Douglas firs and Ponderosa pines. The design of the park was somewhat progressive, offering a limited number of accessible trails. We decided to take a trail marked as handicap accessible for part of the way - our first hike in years. We were wearing slickers and I had rain boots on. It was probably not the best time of year to visit the Peninsula: everything was brilliantly green and very wet.

We were doing fine on a paved path until Frank decided that his trusty motorized chair could make it down the narrower dirt trails, which were not advertised as accessible. I was apprehensive, but stupidly allowed him to continue. It started to pour. The mud was thick and soft. Naturally, the chair got stuck - and there was no one else on the trail. I remember the burden of that moment: it was up to me to spring the chair out of the mud and I hadn't a clue as to how to do it.

I was furious at Frank for being so damn brazen. Not wanting to leave him in such a precarious position to go find help, I found myself at a loss, tears of anger and frustration mixing with rain, like a flash flood, rushing down my face. I wanted to yell at him and tell him it was his fault that he was stuck, but I didn't. He knew. He didn't say anything, didn't complain or show any sign of fear. He just went into his problem solving mode, easing up on the controls, trying to turn the wheels around.

Frank's risk-taking was matched by his ability to think critically, even when sitting, marooned in a wheel chair. He was somehow able to maneuver the chair in such a way that it budged enough to move, and - after some jostles and jerks - to return him to the safety of our motel. Even in the face of my anger, he could not suppress a big grin. He was quite proud of this adventure and did not hesitate to regale all of us that evening with The Perils of Driving a Wheel Chair on Narrow Forest Trails in the Pouring Rain.

As if that wasn't enough, the next day on a hill, another muddy ditch grabbed the wheels of the chair and pushed it into yet another teetering position. Frank could easily have been dumped onto the road if I hadn't held him and the chair until someone finally came to the rescue. By that time, I was ready to take the chair with him in it and send it careening forth in high gear. But I was also quietly pleased; I knew that Frank was making a spiritual come-back and I couldn't wait for his return. As important a break-through as the trip was for us, I was relieved to get back to our accessible bubble of a home. The regimen from which we were trying to escape suddenly became unexpectedly appealing.

* * * *

Frank died, abruptly and unexpectedly, in the early morning hours after his seventy-first birthday, on November 18th 1998. One of the side effects of our miracle drug Elevil, the drug that had given us a 'future', was that it could cause edema and impair circulation. The cause of death was cardiac arrest, but my brother-in-law Chuck, a doctor, said it sounded more like a pulmonary embolism, a clot - perhaps brought on by the Elevil - that had traveled up into his lungs. I couldn't bring myself to order an autopsy. His body had been through so many invasive procedures during the six years of his injury.

The evening of Frank's birthday, I arrived home late because of a meeting at work. As a birthday gift, I'd bought him a few audio tapes of Andreas Bocelli singing arias. Although it was late, I made scallops and mushrooms, one of his favorite meals. Frank played with Truman a while, but every so often would get out of breath. He had not been feeling well. He'd been having chest spasms that day; had even been timing them, they were so frequent. Mary, his personal care attendant, had noted the times of their occurrence on a little blue slip of paper.

Later that evening, as I was helping him with his pajamas, he became unconscious. I called 911. The paramedics revived him and suggested he go to the hospital. Ordinarily, Frank would be eager to go to the hospital anytime he was out of sorts, but this time he just said that he'd been through this before and that he'd be okay. They helped me get him into bed. During the night I checked on him and helped roll him on his side. I became alarmed when, again, he went into a semi-conscious state. I called 911 again. The paramedics came immediately. This time they lifted him out of bed and onto the floor, and began working on his heart. Truman became agitated at the sight of Frank on the floor and I tried to get him out of the room. I was terrified. The thought that Frank might die hit me. The finality of death - never to see him again, the fear of being left alone – my thoughts were spinning, crowding my head. What would I do if he should leave me? We'd been together for 28 years. I called my sister Virginia, and then called Mary.

Although it was after midnight, Mary came over immediately and drove me to the hospital, after the ambulance had taken him. As soon as I arrived, one of the paramedics who'd answered my call took me aside and very gently told me Frank had died, then took me to see him. I kissed him, but his face was already cold and stiff. My brother Ray and my sister-in-law Joan showed up at the hospital; Virginia had called them. I felt bad that Ray was there, because I knew he worked the night shift at a tool-making factory in Woburn; he should have been home sleeping, but I was also thankful they'd come.

I felt awful that I had come home so late on Frank's birthday. If only I had made a bigger deal of it; if only I had gotten him a nicer gift; if only the birthday card had said I loved him in big letters instead of a scribble in the corner of the card. Worst of all, if only I had insisted that we go to the hospital when the paramedics first suggested it. I had been glad that Frank had not wanted to go. All he had wanted to do was to go to bed, and that was what I wanted too, to just go to bed.

* * * *

A year after Frank's death, I took a job as Country Director for the U.S. Peace Corps in the Pacific island nation of Micronesia. My friends thought I was crazy to go live on the other side of the world, all alone, when I had just lost my husband. How to explain that that was why I had to go; that I had 'shut down' after Frank's injury? Although we had succeeded in carving out new roles within our marriage, I had done so by anesthetizing myself so as not to feel too much. Sometimes I felt as if my head were wrapped like a mummy in a gauzy coating that kept me from disintegrating. My eyes could only absorb color in muted shades; my ears, sound in minor tones. There are often conflicting feelings in mourning, even when the person mourned for is someone you've loved deeply. When he's also someone who's been physically dependent on you, there is guilt at feeling relief from the chores of attending him and eagerness to experience new-found freedom – at least that's how it was for me. Yes, I was anxious to get away, to go somewhere far and different. There was an urgency to flee; tomorrow might be too late.

It wasn't until I came to Pohnpei, one of the four major islands of the Federated States of Micronesia, that I could appease my desires and, unexpectedly, could reflect upon my loss. I began to write about Frank, the injury, and its effects on both of us. Writing gave me perspective, understanding, even forgiveness – of myself.

It's not so much that time heals all wounds as that it allows you a space to grow new roots where the old ones were untimely truncated. For me, these new roots did not sprout during my two years in the Pacific but for sure, Micronesia provided the fertilizer. I learned that peace of mind is not about changing your geography. What ails you inside can't really be fixed by an external change of venue. I knew that I was still in some kind of arrested existence. As tranquil and salutary as it was to live in the Pacific, I began to count the days when I could reclaim my roots back on Winthrop Bay.

RETROSPECTIVE - JAY

In the middle of the night, give me Beethoven
In darkness' tumult
Beethoven accompanied him
to precipice and gorge of night journey

they would have known each other
these two men, such irony in their lives
the deaf composer
the disabled advocate for the handicapped
both travelers,
to passion's outer reaches

how suddenly Frank's moods could change
from helpless laughter to grief within grief,
rage, cynicism, determination, despair

he met terror
when his immobile body
tumbled from uncertain hands,
lay, neglected, in unremitting pain

but always
he returned
to reflection, curiosity, insight

I reveled in
his unrestricted space
of mind as
in night's realm,
we coursed
life's outer reaches

I loved
the vigor
of our talks
cynical, probing
partnered or countered
fair and foul

I miss his black humor
his challenge,
one-on-one,
raucous laughter
things knocked over,
tipped upside down
to prove
the marrow of the matter,
his willingness
to seize the issue,
no holds barred.

I miss
the part of me
that's gone with him
as I cherish
the part
that's left behind

AURA'S PERSPECTIVE:
AURA'S PERSPECTIVE: CODA

A few months after my return home from Micronesia, I met an old friend for dinner at the Red Fez, a Middle-Eastern restaurant in the increasingly tone-y South End section of Boston. My friend Jane had been in Los Angeles for the last six months. Her son Paul, who lived out there, had had a devastating motorcycle accident that had left him paraplegic. She'd be returning to LA shortly and so it was lovely to go out to dinner with her and another good friend, Barbara. Having gone through the experience of Frank's injury, I felt there was much I could tell Jane about, but I didn't want to assume that my experience would be hers.

We ordered stuffed grape leaves, hummus, falafel and baba ganoush, drank pinot noir and talked about the changes the Big Dig had brought about in Boston. We discussed the up-coming presidential primaries; all of us shared a great sense of frustration with the Bush administration and an urgency to replace it before irreparable damage was wrought. Barbara, never the shy one, pushed the discussion to Jane's and my mutual experience of dealing with disability. So, how was Paul doing? What *did* this all mean for Jane's future? Would she be moving out to the West Coast permanently?

Jane told us how upbeat and positive Paul, who was in his early thirties, had been during the dark days following the accident.

He'd continued to take charge of renovations he was having done to his house. As children, her three sons had dealt with their father's disability - he was blind. (Although Jane and Bill had been divorced for many years, Bill was still very much a part of their sons' lives.) Bill's condition, she felt, had prepared them; disability wasn't just something that happened to other people, nor was it a subject they were unequipped to discuss openly. They were no strangers to the extra lengths a family needed to take, to accommodate a disabled member and his extraordinary needs. They had found little fault with Paul's hospitalization and were now working on the next steps of his therapy. There seemed to be smooth transition from one phase of the process to the next.

Barbara commented that Frank's relationship with the hospital had been more negative, more confrontational. I quickly countered that that was not the case; that while admittedly he had suffered great frustration and pain because of personnel and institutional shortcomings, there had been many encounters with hospital staff that had overwhelmed him with affirmation and support. I found myself trying to explain Frank's complex reactions, but at the same time not wanting to intrude on Jane with whatever it was that we had gone through, and so I said little.

As I drove home, I felt that I had not done justice to Frank and the complexity of his impressions, observations and feelings about his injury and hospitalization. I was a bit upset with myself for not correcting what I believed was a wrong impression of Frank as a glass-half-empty kind of guy. Yes, Frank was a challenger, a questioner, someone who was always going to ask the hard questions and look behind the curtain to see whether there was indeed a wizard sitting there. All his life he'd been challenging the status quo, be it where his kids went to school, or in the marines, or at Boston University. He would go on to try and change the culture of the hospital: to argue for inclusion of patients in their own individual therapy plans; to insist that a rehab hospital, in particular, should have the goal of minimizing dependency by ensuring access to nurse's call buttons, bed buttons and even elevator buttons. A hospital bureaucrat might muse that Frank was out to "push all the hospital's buttons," literally and, figuratively. An astute observer and activist, Frank was good at railing at the ossification of institutional rules when they were no longer applicable, or only applicable to a few. But he was not simply a curmudgeon who liked to tear down – he would not hesitate to wax eloquently about nurses and therapists who were creative and caring. He reflected on the closeness he felt to therapists and nurses, many of whom resonated to his radical views about rehabilitation.

Perhaps his dedication to working on issues of equality and inclusion for disabled people made him all the more intolerant of the hospital's shortcomings. At the same time, the mindless rules, the lack of sensitivity and awareness, the threatened and guarded negative responses to his questions on the part of the hospital administration, the agonizing pain and the life sentence of dependency, all wore Frank's defenses down. These tsunami-like forces converged, sweeping him away, causing him to lose his grip on the Frank he had once been. He was in no position to fight on his own behalf, let alone fight for all the patients who were trapped in their alienation. He would see himself as McMurphy in *One Flew Over the Cuckoo's Nest*, struggling unsuccessfully to pull back the hospital curtains and expose the smelly bedpans. The challenge of his devastating injury, excruciating pain and complete dependency, were insurmountable even for someone as strong and insightful as Frank.

Before his futile efforts to change hospital policies caused an irretrievable breakdown, I had to step in. It was clear that the role he had played on my behalf, encouraging me to find my own strength and sense of identity, was now the role I would adamantly play for him. I became his zealous advocate. As a couple, our lives had been interwoven. After his injury, we had the unbearable task of unraveling these intricate patterns. It would take many tears, anger, frustration and love to reweave the cloth, but reweave, we did - the texture was different, but it held together.

There were times I was struck by the person I had become, the good and the bad. Traits I was sure were immutably me, disappeared, while new ones I had thought belonged to others, moved in permanently. I knew, in an abstract sort of way, that calamitous events could cause fundamental change, but it was shocking to see it happening to Frank and me. Once, I told Frank that Seth and Anelisa had inherited his athleticism. He looked at me and said that *that* Frank no longer existed. I was surprised and puzzled by his response. Change happens, catastrophic accident or not. We wake up one morning, look into the mirror and wonder, how did we get so gray; we thumb through the photo albums to recapture the children when they were young. But it happens so gradually, we get used to it without even noticing it happening. A catastrophic accident throws that all into high relief. For us, it was abrupt and glaring and deceived us into thinking that we were no longer who we had been. As transforming as change is, it cannot deny what preceded; to do so would be to negate the inter-connected dynamism that is life, making it instead like a very slowed-down cartoon reel, each clip unrelated to the other.

AND SO I MOURN FOR YOU AGAIN - AURA

Six years ago I mourned
when you lay frightened without wings.
The horror of your fate
coexisted with a yearning
for the you that was no longer:

the avid athlete, gliding
on black ice
agile as a great blue heron
taking off;
the curious adventurer,
camping on Aegean beaches
touring West Bank villages
bird watching on salt flats
in Puerto Rico.

I wanted your frozen arms to
embrace me and assure me
all would be well
but they lay beside you
motionless as
a kneeling congregation.
Your effervescence,
Like uncapped soda, had gone flat.

Jay Clark and Aura Sanchez Garfunkel

Into the abyss of grief and pain you fell
but like the hero-with-a-thousand faces,
you came back with the bounty;
like the Buddha under the Bodhi tree,
you came to see what those of us
with working limbs
may never:
how sacred each breath is.

You soared, exhilarated by
re-learning how to ski,
by sailing Narragansett Bay
and with your black lab Truman,
at your side, set out each day
on conquests that would awe
The great explorers.

Your triumphs made my mourning
Seem so wrong
Out of catacombs
you re-emerged,
each day became a holy day.

Now, no Lazarus revival -
no resurrection
and so I mourn for you again, my love
and hope that in your quick, unbearable
departure
you left to us
some of your courage,
your iconoclasm,
your valiant audacity.

Aura and Jay, Winthrop, 2010